Hotwife

A Couple's Guide to Hotwifing

MARISA RUDDER

Marisa Rudder

Author of *Love & Obey*, *Real Men Worship Women,* and *Oral Sex for Women*

**© 2020 Marisa Rudder.
All rights reserved**

© 2020 Marisa Rudder All rights reserved. No part of this publication may be reproduced, distributed, or transmitted in any form or by any means, including photocopying, recording, or other electronic or mechanical methods, without the prior written permission of the publisher, except in the case of brief quotations embodied in critical reviews and certain other noncommercial uses permitted by copyright law. For permission requests, write to the author below.

Available on Amazon Books.

Please contact: Marisa Rudder
Email: femaleledrelationshipbook@gmail.com

Printed in the United States of America Publisher's Cataloging-in-Publication data

ISBN # 978-1-7361835-5-7

Dedication

I would like to dedicate this book to all the strong, brave ladies who have joined or about to join the *Love & Obey* movement and live a female led lifestyle and the supportive gentlemen who recognized the natural superiority of females. It is also my desire that women and men experience the joy, happiness, and passion from exploring all aspects of a loving Female Led Relationship (FLR) and understanding all the benefits of loving female authority. If you have not already, please join us on social media.

You can find out more at our website
http://www.loveandobey.com

Or follow me on social media:

FACEBOOK
https://www.facebook.com/femaleledrelationships

TWITTER
https://twitter.com/loveandobeybook

YOUTUBE
https://www.youtube.com/channel/UCkX3wmd934WR1o3hStbzbiQ

INSTAGRAM
https://www.instagram.com/femaleledrelationships

WARNING

This book contains adult sexual content. It should not be read by anyone under the age of 18 years. In addition to sexually explicit and descriptive content, this book contains controversial sexual discussions about hotwifing, open marriage, threesomes, and polyamorous practices, as well as the female led lifestyle. Be advised that once you open the door to female authority and a female led lifestyle, there is usually no turning back.

Introduction

How do you feel when you see a gorgeous woman? Someone who is sexy, confident, glowing, poised, intelligent, and irresistible? It's very difficult to ignore a woman who captures your attention like this. This is how a husband feels when his wife is desirable, hence the term hotwife. These men are so affected by the attention their hotwives command that they are sexually turned on when other men find her desirable and when she flirts or engages sexually with them.

As strange and scary as this may seem to those who feel this lifestyle falls outside the realm of normalcy for relationships or marriages, hotwifing is becoming one of the most fascinating sexual activities with growing interest in it from both men and women.

At 280,000 searches a month on Google in North America alone, hotwifing is exploding and gaining tremendous interest. After investigating the habits of many couples involved in this lifestyle, I have come to appreciate the various reasons why people are obsessed. I also have a much deeper understanding of how hotwifing can transform a relationship or marriage. Even researchers agree that couples who act on their desires feel liberated because they can be honest about their sexual fantasies, which leads to more open communication than couples in normal relationships.

Everything is changing. What was once a major taboo is becoming much more mainstream, and as controversial as it is, hotwifing is here to stay. Netflix's new show *Monarca* shows a married couple engaging a third person to satisfy both the wife's and husband's needs. Since she is the object of desire, the scene depicts what would be considered a normal interaction during hotwifing. If it's already become a part of a popular Netflix series and mainstream media, interest in hotwifing will only explode.

Today, relationships are dramatically different than they were 20 years ago. The divorce rate is still around 50 percent and infidelity, lying, and dishonesty play a huge role in the destruction of many families, relationships, and marriages. But what if this could all change. What if you could be open to your partner's desires and prioritize happiness for both of you? What if couples could feel completely at ease discussing their needs and desires openly without judgment? Could there be fewer arguments and sneaking around? Could there be more intimacy and sharing rather than jealousy? I have witnessed couples who have reported a complete turnaround in the relationship with open, honest communication and a willingness to try new things. There is a definite interest in trying to change the status quo for relationships, and you will see why hotwifing is turning into an attractive alternative.

A hotwife is a woman who is married or in a long-term relationship but her husband or primary partner takes pleasure in watching her flirt, go on dates, or have sex with others. Traditionally, it's a man who encourages his wife or girlfriend to interact with another man or woman, which he fully supports. There have been many ways in which hotwifing is executed in a relationship. In the past, a man would be ridiculed for the assumption that he was unable to perform during sex, leading his partner to seek out another man to satisfy her. She would be known as an adulterer for cheating on her husband, which leads to disastrous consequences in the relationship.

Today, however, hotwifing is much more complex because women are taking the lead and making the decisions about it in relationships. The first rule of a Female Led Relationship is to focus on the Queen's pleasure. So, when Queens are driving this trend and interest in hotwifing, men are expected to respect it and cater to her. Lucky for them, they already have a ready and willing wife who is more than enthusiastic about being a hotwife.

Hotwifing is much more than just having sex with another person and requires establishing several rules for everything to go smoothly. Many critics believe that hotwifing is a woman's way of cheating on her man and getting him to agree with it. But, as you will see, there are so many more complex issues at play here and hotwifing can take on various forms for different couples. It will be very important that if you are here to explore hotwifing, then you must do so with an open mind. It would be beneficial to explore it openly right alongside your partner to ensure there is no misunderstanding.

I was once a critic of hotwifing and any consensual non-monogamy, as I believed that engaging with a third person and introducing them into the relationship would cause a rift and lead to breakups and divorce. I also felt that hotwifing also goes against monogamy, which has been the gold standard for relationships.

This book will provide a guide for hotwifing and the rules that you will need to follow to be successful. I will also cover how to start hotwifing and how to avoid the common pitfalls. This book will also offer the female perspective since the Queen is in charge and makes the decisions in a Female Led Relationship. Maybe you're a woman who is interested in adding hotwifing to your current sexual activities? How do you reassure your man and execute it successfully? Maybe you're a man who wants your wife or girlfriend to engage in hotwifing. How do you introduce it?

This book may shock many, as hotwifing remains controversial since many couples still believe monogamy is the only way. My hope is that it will open people's minds that having an "open relationship" with others is much more than the sex acts. It is about the issues of trust, honesty, agreements, boundaries, and communication, which are crucial to maintaining a happy and successful relationship of any type. I will attempt to create a structure for couples to enjoy hotwifing and make it a positive experience, one which can enhance and increase your love, trust, and honesty.

Today, more than 50 percent of couples have a cheating spouse, and many end in divorce, so the old, traditional ways are not working. Blame new lifestyles, a society that wants instant pleasure, or a change in values. But something has to change. Hotwifing could be an answer to some of the issues leading to infidelity. The impacts of this new lifestyle include less lying, deceit, and dishonesty by their lovers and life partners, whether married or in a committed relationship.

A relationship that is exciting, loving, honest, and filled with trust should be the new standard. No matter the controversy, hotwifing is here to stay. This book offers a guide on how to engage in it while maintaining a strong bond with your Queen. It is my hope that both men and women will gain tremendous insight into this world which can lead to safe and happy exploration. This should be an adventure that you do together with consent from all parties involved.

Table of Contents

Introduction v

Chapter 1: What Is Hotwifing? 1

Chapter 2: Hotwifing and Non-Monogamy 6

Chapter 3: History of Hotwifing 10

Chapter 4: Women and Sex at Different Ages 15

Chapter 5: Why Do Couples Like Hotwifing? 18

Chapter 6: What Makes a Hotwife Special? 25

Chapter 7: Are Women More Likely to Cheat? 28

Chapter 8: Does Hotwifing Improve a Relationship? 32

Chapter 9: Hotwifing and Desire 37

Chapter 10: Hotwifing and Female Led Relationships 39

Chapter 11: Is HotWifing the Same as Cuckolding? 42

Chapter 12: Is Hotwifing the Same as Polyamory? 46

Chapter 13: Why Does the Bull Like hotwifing? 49

Chapter 14: How to Choose the Right Bull 51

Chapter 15: How to Turn Your Wife into a Hotwife 57

Chapter 16: What Are the Rules and Boundaries? 60

Chapter 17: Types of Hotwifing Solo Hotwife..................... 65

Chapter 18: The First Hotwifing Encounter 71

Chapter 19: Creating Perfect Hotwifing Scenarios 75

Chapter 20: How to Deal with Hesitations.......................... 78

Chapter 21: Avoid Common Pitfalls..................................... 81

Chapter 22: Practicing Safe Sex 85

Chapter 23: How to Deal with Disagreements 88

Chapter 24: Keep the Primary Relationship Alive 96

Chapter 25: A Woman's Needs in an Open Relationship ... 101

Chapter 26: The Rules for a Female Led Relationship........ 104

Chapter 27: Alternative Forms of Hotwifing 110

Conclusion... 114

CHAPTER 1

What Is Hotwifing?

Have you fantasized about watching your wife with other men? Does the thought of knowing she wants and enjoys other men turn you on? Have you thought about asking her to have sex with someone else? Chances are you're interested in hotwifing.

Hotwifing is a practice or fetish in which couples engage in a sexual relationship with a third person. It's different from threesomes because the Queen is engaging in the sex act with or without her husband or partner present, but he is in agreement, and he will often support the activity. Both people are in agreement, and there is consent from the third man or woman. Hotwifing is more of a female led activity because it is the woman engaging in sexual activities with other men; therefore, she is actually in control of what is happening.

In the past, hotwifing was inferred to be completely encouraged by husbands, but today, with women leading relationships, it's the opposite. Hotwifing offers the opportunity for a woman to have complete satisfaction, and let's face it, she's getting all the attention she wants and needs. Hotwifing is different from cuckolding in which the man is purposely made to feel humiliated and is generally incapable of satisfying his Queen. Hotwifing usually has no elements of humiliation because husbands are often secure alpha males who want to put their very attractive and desirable wives or girlfriends on display.

The belief of placing a woman on a pedestal is aligned with the goal of Female Led Relationships where women are worshipped and adored by not only her husband, but others who she chooses to engage with. The Queen decides she wants to be with another man while her husband watches. What's interesting about what happens is that, unlike cheating, both people are in agreement. There is no lying, sneaking around, or ignoring, resulting in many couples enjoying the openness aspect of this. Couples report a great deal of excitement because often, one partner does not feel that he or she has satisfied the other enough sexually, so they openly welcome a third man or woman to ramp up the excitement.

I have received countless letters of objection from mostly men about Hotwifing because men feel that if they openly desire to see their wives with another man, it makes them weak, incapable, and humiliated. But with female led hotwifing, men feel empowered and proud of their Queens, and they view hotwifing as an extra opportunity to prove their loyalty and service to her. The important point about hotwifing is that it removes the stigma associated with having extra and outside sexual partners while in a relationship or marriage.

To the critics who claim that hotwifing is just cheating, I will offer this rebuttal: For centuries, men have tolerated and participated in infidelity where cheating, lying, and sneaking around their women were condoned. There are websites like Ashley Madison set up for cheating, yet when it comes to hotwifing in which men give their consent and often motivate women to do it, other men strongly object. As a writer promoting Female Led Relationships, what a woman wants goes. Period. If a woman wants to engage in hotwifing, in the female led world, *it will happen.*

However, hotwifing is taking on a movement all on its own. At over 280,000 searches on Google a month, there are hundreds of thousands of websites devoted to hotwifing, and there is no doubt that it is growing with no end in sight. Today, you can find parties, events, and mainstream clubs in multiple cities in North America that promote hotwifing. At one point, having a threesome was at the top of men's fantasies for decades and there was never any criticism or condescension about it.

Threesomes have been depicted in hundreds of movies and videos, not to mention the number of porn videos that have made threesome and group sex action an accepted activity. Hotwifing is different because the woman is in control. She is the center and main attraction, not some side dish to be added to the play. In this regard, a Queen who wants to be a hotwife has the advantage of doing so, right alongside her spouse and any other consenting adult.

There are numerous reasons why couples enjoy hotwifing and open relationships. But one of the driving factors is that today, with women in charge and leading in many relationships, the woman decides that she wants to be satisfied by another man who may be better at sex and more well-endowed. Whether this is deemed to be shocking, controversial, or downright wrong by the critics, more couples are engaging in hotwifing and are from all walks of life.

In the media, hotwifing has become mainstream. In the Emmy nominated show *Succession* on Netflix, Shiv Roy has her husband sign a contract in which it is understood that she will be having sex with other men. Another Netflix series, *Monarca* blatantly promoted hotwifing as an essential part of the married couple's life. Hotwifing has been a central theme in the hit series *House of Cards,* specifically when Claire takes a younger lover while her husband was fully aware and supported the activity. Today, more young couples have admitted to engaging in hotwifing on a regular basis with no issues with the main relationship, and there are dozens of sites dedicated to it.

Wealthy couples often used hotwifing where the man was much older than the woman and got to the age where he was unable to perform, but instead of feeling humiliated or made to do some demeaning act, he felt empowered to partake and watch his Queen. In these types of relationships, men often participate in finding their wife's bull and will watch their sex act. This book will focus on hotwifing from the female perspective. However, if you are a man who wants to introduce it to your Queen, this will also help her to get excited about it knowing that the activity is female-driven with supportive participation.

In Female Led Relationships, the man's responsibility under his submission to the female's complete and absolute authority over him is to allow her freedom, so she can achieve happiness and as much pleasure as possible in her life. Hotwifing is best approached in a similar manner to the *Love & Obey* philosophy where the woman is the Queen and her man is the supportive gentleman who is making all of her fantasies, including hotwifing, come true. Why is this so important? Because a woman's happiness in a relationship is mandatory.

The saying "Happy Wife, Happy Life" is true for this very reason. I believe that a man showing his highest commitment to the happiness of his Queen by indulging in all of their fantasies allows for mutual exploration, which leads to evolution. Most couples who engage in hotwifing have confirmed that this activity was a game changer, deepening the bond in the primary relationship, allowing for more honesty and open communication, while allowing women and men to support their evolution.

This book is going to take you on a journey to explore female sexuality, sexual freedom, learning how to spice up your relationship or marriage, and deal with obstacles that may have been holding back your relationship or marriage from being successful. It will present concepts of open relationships and consensual non-monogamy, in the hope of shedding light on how something considered dysfunctional can be a game changer in dating, relationships, and marriages.

Chapter 2

Hotwifing and Non-Monogamy

Hotwifing falls under consensual non-monogamy and ethical non-monogamy. Consensual non-monogamy involves couples who are married or in long-term relationships but seek to have external sexual encounters with the permission and agreement of their primary partner. So, you and your Queen are married, but you make a decision to explore mostly casual encounters with others. There is understanding, agreement, and consent from all involved. Consensual non-monogamy encompasses open relationships, swinging, polyamory cuckolding, and hotwifing. And while consensual non-monogamy has become a hot topic, with examples cropping up everywhere in media, politics, and celebrities, the practice of a couple staying together but seeking outside physical, romantic, or emotional coupling is nothing new.

Jessica Fern, a psychologist, found that as of September 2020, about 4 percent of Americans, nearly 16 million people, are "practicing a non-monogamous style of relationship," and other studies show that over 21 percent of Americans engaged in consensual non-monogamy at "some point in their lifetime." In January 2020, a poll found that about one-third of US adults believe that their ideal relationship is non-monogamous to some degree.

Let's face it, we all have sexual fantasies, and sometimes we want to act on them, even when those crushes and fantasies aren't about our partner or spouse. Most of the time, we ignore our fantasies, which can go unfulfilled. For many, cheating is the only option. However, consensual non-monogamy now seems like a better option because there is more honesty and openness, and in many cases, long-term relationships and marriages remain intact. Those who engage in CNM agree on their relationship rules ahead of time, and they allow each other to have romantic and sexual relationships with others. Thus, CNM differs from monogamy in that there is a firm agreement and open acceptance to have some form of extra outside romantic or sexual relationships while maintaining the integrity of the primary marriage or relationship.

People who seem to engage in CNM tend to have active imaginations, a preference for variety, and a proclivity to engage in new experiences. They hold more positive attitudes toward non-monogamy and a greater willingness to engage in these types of open relationships. There is no evidence that they are dysfunctional, unhappy, or affected by past trauma. Non-monogamy is growing. People in consensual non-monogamous relationships report relatively high levels of trust, honesty, intimacy, and satisfaction, as well as relatively low levels of jealousy in their relationships.

Ethical monogamy was derived out of the desire to change non-monogamy from being associated with the negative connotations associated with infidelity and cheating. Will Smith and Jada Pinkett are just one celebrity couple of hundreds who publicly spoke about their consensual non-monogamous marriage, and today, they are still happily married. Other celebrities who admitted to enjoying the lifestyle are Gwyneth Paltrow, Jessica Biel, and Thomas Middleditch.

Why are couples obsessed with hotwifing and consensual non-monogamy? Couples report strong feelings of connection along with excitement and sexual satisfaction after engaging in sex with additional partners. They also experience more intimacy and appreciation for their partner along with more trust and openness after a shared open relationship experience. They are relieved that nothing has to remain secretive or in the dark ever again. This opens often leads to a renewed sense of trust, closeness, and togetherness, all of which are hugely beneficial for the long-term health of any relationship.

Couples also report much more passionate sex when they were alone together after their outside experience. One of the biggest complaints of most relationships is the lack of sex, the decline in the quality of sex, and overall boredom with sex. Most couples who practice open relationships have been together for years, and hotwifing, threesomes, or more often helps keep the excitement alive even when the couple is by themselves. Most people don't have outside relationships all the time, and typically people have one once in a while. Maybe that is once a month, once a quarter, or even once a year. However, that sexual freedom is with you every day and makes the sex you have with your primary partner so much more thrilling. Perhaps you talk about it to get in the mood, or even while you are having sex with each other. Let's face it, human beings are always searching for more. Therefore, more excitement in a relationship is important. Open relationships breathe new and exciting life into a relationship that, while loving and committed, may feel a bit boring and stale. The voyeuristic and taboo nature of hotwifing, or whatever you have chosen to do, creates a cool, kinky vibe for some couples and opens endless possibilities for exciting, titillating, and highly satisfying sexual experiences together.

Scientists Ellen Berscheid and Elaine Walster suggest that there are two types of love, one based more on passion and another that is more about companionship. Passionate love was always thought to fizzle out fast or become less fiery, and more like a friendship instead. You hear that the "honeymoon is over" and the relationship becomes less exciting. However, companionship and love marked by commitment, intimacy, and a sharing of interests tends to be less intense and can lack elements of sexual desire and attraction.

Perhaps, as a result, this type of love tends to be only moderately satisfying, leading individuals to want to spice up the relationship and pursue non-monogamy. Hotwifing represents a mixture of the two. The primary relationship offers companionate love, while the sexual encounters with additional partners represent passionate love. Most people require both, and in the pursuit of more excitement, sexual adventure, and satisfaction, couples are choosing to explore hotwifing.

Chapter 3

History of Hotwifing

The history of hotwifing dates back to medieval times, so it is not new. Hotwifing appears in literature as early as the 13th century. In *The Merchant's Tale*, by Geoffrey Chaucer, a rich old bachelor, January, decides it's finally time to get married and settles on an eighteen-year-old girl named May as his ideal wife. Chaucer gives the details of the wedding night—the physical discrepancy between wrinkled old January lusting after May, a beautiful, young woman. January's hotwifing arrives in the form of a younger man, Damian.

Soon, the old man goes blind, which makes him even more jealous, and finally, May concocts an elaborate scheme to meet her would-be lover in the garden, with her husband waiting oblivious and blind nearby.

In classical mythology, the maenads, or followers of Dionysus or Bacchus, frenziedly tore Orpheus apart. Dolled up in fawn-skins, wine-fueled, and brandishing their long sticks wreathed in ivy and tipped with a pinecone, the maenads were uncontrollable on a night out. In the 17th century, women were often seen as more lascivious than men, their passions ruled by nature rather than reason.

Nineteenth-century physiologists clung to this notion that women were governed more by nature than by civilized thought. But they fiddled around with the concept of female nature, adjusting it to preconceptions about social class. They argued that women—at least the decent middle-class sort—were pure at heart and not driven by physical passion in the way that men were.

Lower-class women might be perceived as more physical and in touch with their animal nature than middle-class ones. Patriarchy suggested this was the reason middle or upper-class men turned to prostitutes. It could even be suggested that men could relieve their lusts on one group (consisting of prostitutes) without compromising the virtue of "respectable" females.

During the Renaissance, from the 16th to the 18th centuries, Europe had a cultural obsession with hotwifing. Women were believed to be more lustful than men, largely because they were subject to the whims of their womb, which was believed to move independently around a woman's body, causing her to lose control.

In medieval times, one of the reasons for hotwifing was the passing down of property to heirs. Women were to get pregnant and have children to continue the lineage or kingdom. It was not uncommon that in the event a man could not perform his duties because of age or illness, women might have to engage with an outside lover. Again, the theme of "survival."

Hotwifing has existed in wealthy circles for decades. When a much older man marries a younger woman and is unable to perform, it is understandable that she will take a younger lover from time to time, and her husband will happily go along and support the effort to find a suitable man. He may even be enthusiastically showing off his wife to other men and watching or engaging with them during sexual activities.

Today, in many popular shows, hotwifing is seen in shows like *House of Cards* where Robin Wright's character Kate as the first lady openly cuckolds with a younger man with the consent of her husband, Frank, as well as in the show *Succession* on Netflix. The character Shiv Roy has her husband sign a contract that includes a clause of him accepting that she will be sleeping with other men.

In a recent interview with CNN, clinical psychologists David Ley, Ph.D., Justin Lehmiller, Ph.D., and sex advice columnist Dan Savage shared the findings of a national survey they conducted.

In preparation for his own book, Lehmiller surveyed thousands of Americans and found that 58 percent of men had fantasies about hotwifing. To be clear, this means they fantasize about their partner having sex with someone else, either while they watch or while they're somewhere else. Lehmiller stated that "men are more likely to fantasize about hotwifing, and they do it more often. But there are several women who have these fantasies as well, which points to the need for more research focused on women's hotwifing desires. These survey results show that, unlike before, hotwifing fantasies can be about sexual liberation and empowerment, which mirrors my own feedback from thousands of couples worldwide.

Hotwifing has raised the discussion on the suppression of female sexuality, which can be considered one of the most detrimental interventions of western culture. Research has shown that the female sex drive is stronger than that of the male, and it posed a powerful threat to the stability of social order. For civilized society to develop, suppressing female sexuality was necessary. So much so that countless women have lived their lives with far less sexual pleasure than they would have enjoyed in the absence of this large-scale suppression. One of the biggest socializing influences was the Catholic Church, which is ironic as many of their hidden crimes have surfaced involving sexual harassment and pedophilia.

However, the structure of the Catholic Church is such that women have no power and are subject to the oppression of the males. Other institutions aimed at suppressing female sexuality include the legal system, corporations, and parenting. The fact is that society has condoned and maintained a double standard of sexual morality by condemning certain sexual activities by women while permitting identical actions for men. I believe that suppression of female sexuality has led to very little research conducted for a long time as well as the biases involved in studies done on female sexual experience, sexual organs, and female reproductive health.

Research done by Baumeister and Twenge proposes two main theories. The first is the male control theory in which women's sexuality are suppressed to guard them against other males, thereby ensuring paternity certainty and eliminating sperm competition to ensure children are indeed his and he is not fathering another man's child.

The second is the social exchange theory in which other women are critics of female sexuality as a way of maintaining the reward system. For instance, a woman uses her sexuality for status and securing a man. If women offer sex more freely, its exchange value will decrease, and the average woman would get lesser from the exchange than she would've gotten had sex offered by women been more scarce. Some feminists have also argued for a female control theory with men seeking to suppress female sexuality as a way of controlling them and keeping them impoverished and needy. If women were allowed to freely engage in sex with men, a husband would have no way of controlling women or the household.

Today, all women are allowed to freely explore their sexuality. Hotwifing not only demonstrates how women's confidence, feelings of empowerment, and dominance is transforming the female led activity from being what was once forced upon women as their duty to keep husbands happy to now being the newest expression of female dominance in the relationship and marriage.

Chapter 4

Women and Sex at Different Ages

As part of understanding hotwifing, we need to look at women's experience of sex and sexual intimacy at different ages and phases of life. People often think that women only seem keen to have sex when they're younger and as far as their mid-thirties. This is a complete misconception as women describe having the desire for sex throughout all phases of life. The only difference is that the type of sex and the interaction can change. During their 20s, women are more likely to have fun, sexy, short adventures with lots of experimentation.

By their 30s, women avoid sexually explicit overtures and are often looking for a serious relationship rather than sex. Their goal is long-term monogamous commitment. But during this time, many women begin to open up and explore even more than their 20s as they learn to be comfortable with what they like and don't like. They are more confident in their interactions with men and they are much more assertive in how, when, and where they will have sex. This can be an incredible time of much higher sexual arousal and the desire for more sex, even in a relationship or marriage.

In their 40s and with maturity, women tend to have a higher quality of sex, focusing on deeper connections, more interesting positions, and better orgasms. They're no longer after the high of multiple conquests but much more about a more satisfying experience with their primary partner. The responsibilities with work, children, and household chores can pose a major challenge, and sometimes the frequency of sex can go decline during this time, but being in longer-term relationships or marriages means the time to develop greater sexual intimacy. Often both men and women are more secure in their relationships where they can explore open relationships, hotwifing, cuckolding, and a variety of alternative forms of sexual interactions.

This appears to be one reason women, beginning in their late 30s and 40s, begin to enjoy hotwifing. Spontaneous and responsive are two distinct kinds of desire. Both are normal. Being overcome by sexy thoughts while scrubbing the kitchen floor or walking by an attractive person is a spontaneous desire. It happens for about 15 percent of women. Responsive desire shows up after sexy things are already happening. This happens for 30 percent of women and is how women experience desire later in life. This also explains why once a woman is turned on to hotwifing, she decides to explore it, and her desire for these types of encounters grows.

In their 50s, women are still having sex, but bodies are changing, and so are relationships. There are also new concerns like keeping jobs, financial security in retirement, and keeping marriages and long-term relationships strong. But despite these challenges, women still desire to be desired and have sex. The sex may be more focused on greater intimacy and connecting emotionally, as well as a little less frenzied and experimental. Women may begin to lose a bit of interest in frequent sex with a bit of loss of libido as they go through menopause, but they are still interested in being desirable to men. Many women may be divorced or unmarried, but sex still plays a role in their lives. And because of their experience, it tends to be much more focused on doing what brings them the most pleasure. There's less need to try this and try that and more of a focus on having a wonderful night or experience.

In their 50s, couples tend to have more discretionary income so they can splurge on vacations, upscale clubs, or fancier dinners and locations for sex. This is a bonus. The sexual experience for women can change dramatically, but it's alive and well. In their 60s, women still have sex, but its gentler and more focused on connection. At this age, sex is about "making love" and engaging in an act that is frequently more about maintaining intimacy than it is about animal instinct. They are no longer sexually impulsive and do not enter relationships for the sake of a sexual or romantic partnership.

Women are sexual and interested in sex throughout their lifetimes, but the goals of sex and intimacy may change at different ages. As a woman matures and a couple is more secure in the relationship or marriage, the more they will be interested in exploring hotwifing and other types of open relationships. A maturing woman also becomes more confident in what they desire in a sexual interaction, and as they take control in the relationship. they begin to demand better opportunities for sexual satisfaction. Most men will tend to introduce the concept of hotwifing to women, but they tend to take the reins leading the activities, and eventually, they tend to drive the desire for it.

Chapter 5

Why Do Couples Like Hotwifing?

Why do couples like hotwifing? Your Queen gets to have variety, excitement, and sexual satisfaction with her husband or supportive gentleman's approval. You feel a real desire to see her desired by others, and she gets to be the center of attention. Let's face it, most relationships are difficult, and today, there are so many cases where couples are looking for ways to spice up the relationship. We all like variety. Women love wearing a variety of outfits, shoes, and bags. Men love driving different cars, going to various bars. Some people love being around people of varying nationalities or trying different foods—people want variety and I believe that they need it in their relationships.

As the leader of the female led movement where women are taking control of the relationship, I have noticed how receptive people are to this change in power. Men are requesting it and women are loving it. Many couples are changing the dynamic in relationships because they are looking for variety and many are looking to fulfill inner needs. There are very few relationships that break up over hotwifing. But 50 percent of traditional marriages still end in divorce. It's a fact that fewer couples in Female Led Relationships divorce. That suggests that even though this is a radical movement, there could be something about it that bonds people in a relationship.

Research shows that 4 to 5 percent of Americans have agreed to have an open relationship. In other words, they've given their consent not to be monogamous. The National Opinion Research Center's General Social Survey revealed that more than 20 percent of married men and nearly 15 percent of married women admit to infidelity, a number that's risen almost 40 percent for women in the past 20 years. In addition, some studies have found that between 30 and 60 percent of married individuals in the United States will engage in adultery at some point in their marriage. So, while only 4 to 5 percent of men and women are choosing to be open about their extramarital relations, somewhere between 15 and 60 percent are opting for a less consensual form of infidelity.

Hotwifing is not infidelity and is done with consent and together. In life, most people engage in hotwifing and they don't even realize it. Women post semi-nude pics on social media showing off their bikini bodies, while millions of men are checking them out and most likely masturbating to them. No one cares. Boyfriends and husbands are encouraging the posting of racy pictures and videos daily. So, this is a version of hotwifing. It's the first step. She is showing off her beauty and attractiveness and men everywhere desire her.

I was most shocked to see how many parents on social media and TikTok allow semi-clad pictures of their daughters and videos of them dancing in bikinis, completely aware of the attention from millions of people around the world with no criticism or judgment. So what society accepts as mainstream is changing by the day. Hotwifing is no longer an extreme fetish that people in underground circles engage in, and more couples are excited to add it to their daily lives.

Why Do Men or Women Desire Hotwifing?

Research and psychologists have found that when a man or woman sees their partner with someone else, it can excite them and give them feelings of being proud to be with someone desirable by others. People with attractive partners get this feeling when people pay lots of attention to their husbands, wives, girlfriends, or boyfriends.

Sometimes we all feel good when others want what we have. It's a basic human emotion. As an extension, sometimes, realizing that you cannot sexually fulfill your partner and you would be fine with someone else doing it is also exciting and builds a feeling of trust and control because the partner being cuckolded condoned.

Couples often race home to tell their stories and share the experience openly, with some individuals feeling subservience. This is true in some Female Led Relationships where men will be happy when their Goddess is allowed to choose any man she wants. They get turned on by the sight of seeing another man satisfying his Queen sexually. Pleasure also comes from this being the ultimate show of respect to allow your woman to do what she wants. In a Female Led Relationship, men condone and even encourage their Queen to have sex with another man. Of course, there is an element of taboo and couples gain excitement from participating in the forbidden.

I grew up a very devout Catholic. So much so that I was afraid to steal a pack of gum, much less engage in sex with another man while my partner watched. In my early relationships, I recall flying into a rage if my boyfriend's eye moved to look at another woman. This jealousy and rigid behavior caused me to become incredibly angry and always constantly worried about cheating.

One of my first relationship partners suggested an open relationship, and I can recall being so upset about it that I secretly knew the relationship was done. Once I broke out of these restraints based on religious conditioning, I was free to enjoy relationships and changed my outlook on this subject forever. We must also understand the deeper advantages of hotwifing, which include more trust and a deeper bond between you and your Queen.

Relationships are one of the biggest influences in our lives and can become a curse each day or a new opportunity to explore and gain more enjoyment and happiness. Once you push those boundaries, you are set free. While Hotwifing is new, it's growing. I never thought Ashley Madison would become such a large organization spread across hundreds of countries. I realized that there were millions of people searching for new types of relationships. As much as I have criticized infidelity, I was open to understanding the trends and changes happening in relationships.

Our sexual openness depends on a variety of factors, including security, commitment, fear, jealousy, possessiveness, sense of entitlement, and more, all of which factor into the algorithm that renders our comfort level with sexual openness. Some people are comfortable at orgies, others are only comfortable having sex on camera to make a video that they will later watch. It just so happens that hotwifing is the way that couples can begin to explore these several types of openness with sex.

What's the Advantage to the Queen?

Right from the start, a woman who engages in hotwifing with her partner fully supporting it has the best of both worlds. She is receiving sexual pleasure, which she may not have had previously, and she has her husband or boyfriend serving her like a Queen. So, the woman is ultimately in the power position. Some will criticize, but how a couple chooses to build excitement in their lives is completely up to them. Many couples report a closer bond with their partners because, unlike cheating, they are open and upfront about everything that happens.

With both partners in agreement, the couple can control how far they will take their activities. A satisfied woman is a lot easier to deal with than one who is unsatisfied. There are many reasons why women are left unsatisfied. Take the problem of an abnormally small penis and a larger vagina. It would be impossible for a woman to be satisfied if her partner is unable to satisfy her. Should the relationship break up over this one issue? Or would it be practical to try to solve it in a different way? Sometimes men are impotent and unable to satisfy a woman. I know many who have had to endure this, only to end in disaster. For years, if a woman failed to have sex with her man, many justified a man's need to find a woman outside of the marriage as a mistress.

A majority of men today would still take this route, but if a woman does it and gains approval, it is still condemned. This double standard is fading as more women are demanding what they want and need, and a few have turned to hotwifing. There is not as much research about women participating in hotwifing, but those who do it successfully have said that has made them more assertive and freer. They feel more connected to their sexuality and overall, it improved their desire to have sex more with their man.

What's the Advantage to the Man?

What's the advantage to men? Men indulge in fantasies every day either through their consumption of porn or during intimate times with their partner. Hotwifing can be the real-life fulfillment of a fantasy. Many men desire to see their wives engaging in sex with another man after seeing it in a porn video or reading about it. Sometimes it's a fantasy they have had since early adulthood.

Other times, it's more than that. He wants to show his Queen his devotion. He derives sexual satisfaction from knowing he is in service to his woman, and she is still his Queen. The man still feels like he is in control because he wants to see his Queen with a man who is better able to satisfy her and may even be more well-endowed or more muscular, for his own satisfaction. By desiring to show service and getting involved in directing the activity, it places men in a much more alpha and powerful position than cuckolding, where the goal is humiliation.

Most alpha men still want to serve a powerful woman, and many have a deep desire to show great service to her even though they are strong and powerful in their own lives. Many are CEOs, athletes, or successful entrepreneurs who have no problem taking charge and being aggressive in life. However, in the bedroom, they want to fulfill fantasies, and one happens to be hotwifing. Sometimes, the fantasy is about voyeurism, and he derives pleasure from watching the sex act.

No matter the reason, many men have admitted to being turned on watching their wife or girlfriend with another man or partaking in the activity. In his book *Tell Me What You Want: The Science of Sexual Desire and How It Can Help Improve Your Sex Life*, Justin Lehmiller surveyed thousands of Americans and discovered that 58 percent of men and around 30 percent of women had thought about hotwifing.

Hotwifing often begins in a marriage where the husband derives sexual pleasure from watching his wife have sex with another man, and he partakes as well or simply watches, or she does it alone and they talk about the experience. The hotwife will flirt or engage in sex with other men in front of her husband. This knowledge and acceptance of the wife's sexual activities with other men make the husband in such relationships feel like he is orchestrating the act, like a director.

So, in this way, he still feels empowered to allow his gorgeous partner to be adored and experienced by other men. It is his involvement as the director of the scene that is the key difference for men who enjoy this aspect much more. They can maintain their alpha personalities while the Queen can have the variety she craves because no female led woman is going to be pushed or forced into hotwifing if there isn't something in it for her.

CHAPTER 6

What Makes a Hotwife Special?

What makes a hotwife so special? What sets her apart from other women? Hotwives capitalize on their natural seductiveness. Why save all that sex appeal for home if your husband doesn't mind sharing? A lot of women say that they get a confidence boost from knowing their husband thinks they are irresistible to other men.

Some say the best thing about hotwifing is that the thrill is amplified. First comes the anticipation of play, and the second comes with the actual event. But the biggest excitement for many hotwives comes after the hook-up when they share details with their husbands, or they end up having lustful exciting sex together since they're both so turned on.

We all love to be desired by people who are not our partners. It's a common longing among people who are in monogamous relationships, even happy ones. For many women, it's fun receiving attention at a bar or by chatting online with potential partners and going through the fun parts of the dating ritual with the support of their beloved husbands.

Our culture grants females validation and power based primarily on their sexual appeal to men. Hotwives can fulfill their wildest fantasies and feed their sexual desire without being confined to one sexual partner and ability to explore different bodies as they wish. Many women have admitted to being very reserved during their single years because they want to appear conservative when looking for a partner for a long-term relationship. But once they are secure in a long-term marriage or relationship, hotwifing becomes pure fun.

Hotwifing is empowering. Women feel sexy and free from typical societal limitations and can be appreciated by more than one man. Hot wives are in control of their sexuality, and the attention boosts confidence in and outside of the bedroom. Especially great for those with a high sex drive. Some Queens have reported feeling a unique sense of power when in a room full of potential conquests. They know they can have anyone they want without guilt. One Queen describes the thrill of having the experience of another man, flirting with her while her husband sat on the other side of her, looking on. There was no tension, jealousy, and a feeling of complete ease.

Healthy attention versus toxic attention must be balanced. When women want attention, they often suffer from low self-esteem. Sometimes they feel insecure in the relationship, and they need to feel validated. This can go overboard when all they want is attention and they feel the need to use men for attention. Men can often feel drained and used. However, there is a difference between being used for attention and when she has a genuine need to feel appreciated and demand to be treated like a Queen. Female led women tend to be much more secure, confident, and level-headed. Yes, they know they attract attention, but they are not attention vampires. Hotwifing can be a very exciting adventure for your Queen, but it's important to establish that it should not be done to fuel a toxic or unhealthy need for attention.

One thing to consider is that it is possible for women who love hotwifing to have a histrionic personality disorder. A histrionic personality disorder is one of a group of conditions called dramatic personality disorders. People with these disorders have intense, unstable emotions and distorted self-images. For people with histrionic personality disorder, their self-esteem depends on the approval of others and does not arise from a true feeling of self-worth. They have an overwhelming desire to be noticed and often behave dramatically or inappropriately to get attention. They tend to want lots of attention, and they will dress very provocatively, acting very seductive or flirtatious. Even though these women may seem narcissistic, they may actually enjoy hotwifing because it matches their personality.

CHAPTER 7

Are Women More Likely to Cheat?

Are women more likely to cheat? Institute for family studies research shows that women are more likely to cheat early on but less likely in older age groups. Among married adults ages 18 to 29, women are slightly more likely than men to be guilty of infidelity 11 percent vs. 10 percent. But this gets smaller between 30 to 34 and afterward grows wider in older age groups. Infidelity for both men and women increased during the Middle Ages.

In the 1990s, the infidelity rate peaked among men ages 50 to 59 at 31 percent and women ages 40 to 49 at 18 percent. Between 2000 and 2009, the highest rate of infidelity shifted to older age groups, with men ages 60 to 69 at 29 percent and women ages 50 to 59 at 17 percent. Meanwhile, during the age of 80 plus, infidelity increased from 5 percent to 12 percent.

Men who cheated are more likely than females to be married. Among men who have cheated on their spouse before, 61 percent are currently married, while 34 percent are divorced or separated. However, only 44 percent of women who have cheated before are currently married, while 47 percent are divorced or separated. Other findings uncovered that women aged 35 to 40 were the most likely to dabble in infidelity. One popular reason: Many are childless. They look for love elsewhere out of feelings of neglect, either physical or emotional. If sex becomes, well, kind of boring and predictable, women may wander away to find someone else who can spice things up.

Feeling emotionally undervalued or just flat-out ignored can also lead to infidelity. If a husband is neglecting his wife because of work, nights out with the boys, or other activities, the wife might go on the prowl for a guy who makes her feel good about herself—as opposed to hanging out with a husband who makes her feel less desired and treasured. For women, however, cheating may be evidence of a more thought-out plan to address perceived needs. It is also unclear whether more men simply get caught cheating because women can hide infidelity better.

Sex therapist Candice Cooper-Lovett agrees that women's ability to hide infidelity is at least somewhat adaptive. She says, "A lot of women in my practice have shared that cheating was something that you take to the grave with you because men can't handle cheating in the way that women do or are expected to." Is it because of a desire for more sex? It's an outdated stereotype that men are more into sex than women, and a new, albeit small, study confirms that almost 60 percent of women want more sex than their partner does or can provide.

Therapists report that couples often want to know if they are engaged in enough sex, the right kind and if they should be doing something different in bed. They are concerned with comparing themselves to friends and associates as well as the quantity rather than the quality of the satisfaction they are receiving. This places an unnecessary amount of pressure on constantly being worried that sex is inadequate or not good enough. Searches for "sexless marriage" are 3.5 times more than those for "unhappy marriage" and women tend to be the driving force in the search for answers on why men can't keep up. Women can often confuse men being stressed or experiencing some kind of erectile dysfunction for a lack of interest in them because they are no longer sexy enough. This causes stress for women and corresponding stress for men.

Studies show that infidelity can begin approximately seven years after. Why would most marriages decline after only seven years? Is seven years the amount of time it takes for a woman to get bored of her husband? Does he lose interest after seven years, which consequently makes her lose interest? Some of the reasons could be that perhaps their husbands are not giving them the attention and respect they deserve. Perhaps they still love their men, but the spark has vanished from their marriage. Alternatively, they may decide to have an open relationship to satisfy their physical needs while still sharing a tight emotional bond.

One of the biggest issues cited was the fact that women felt judged by their husbands when they discussed their fantasies, and this did not happen with extramarital affairs where they were engaging with like-minded men. Many cheating scenarios can begin with a friend of the opposite sex. This tends to happen for women. An "innocent" opposite-sex friendship begins to drive a wedge between a married couple. Yet, instead of prioritizing the marriage and ending the friendship, the woman defends the friend.

A couple in a relationship that may be destroyed due to cheating with the friend may not realize that the friend who appears to be innocent, is not without fault. Sometimes the friend meant to drive a wedge between them. Why? Because it's fun. It's how they get their kicks and pass the time. It's how they add a spark to their own relationship or how they find validation in life. Because, thanks to things like texting and social media, it's easy and risk-free. But the fact that cheating can often begin as an innocent friendship and end in a disaster with less regard for the primary relationship is a big reason why cheating and infidelity don't work.

Today, more women are rethinking infidelity. They are admitting that they love their husbands and want to be with them, but they want the freedom of exploring sex with multiple partners. They don't see infidelity as a transgression but a creative act to deal with an institution they'd come to experience as suffocating or oppressive. More and more women are unwilling to abandon the marriages and families they'd built over years or decades through divorce, but they still want their needs to be met.

Never before in history has it become more accepted for women to explore their needs, and this is what I believe is driving the trend of hotwifing. Not only are women demanding this, but men are eager to please the Queen and they also get satisfaction in knowing that they are with a highly desirable and sexual wife. Today's hotwifing is much more of a two-way driven interaction than in the past when the man had to convince his wife to be a hotwife.

The significance of all of this is that hotwifing could very well put an end to cheating. Many men will argue that cuckolding, where the man is often submissive and considered a weak beta male, can never be a viable solution because women will be unable to respect a man who appears weak. However, the difference with hotwifing is that the man maintains his alpha status while there is agreement among all who are involved. There isn't the same broken trust issues, lying, sneaking around, and all the destruction that follows from infidelity.

CHAPTER 8

Does Hotwifing Improve a Relationship?

Does hotwifing improve a relationship? Yes, as long as you address these issues and ask yourselves: Do you trust each other? Are you and your Queen genuine and sincere during good times and bad? Is your sex life healthy? If you can both communicate openly about your desires without fear, you're off to a good start. Hotwifing has been shown to improve a relationship in a variety of ways as noted below.

Improved Communication

Couples who are involved in hotwifing need to communicate. It's important to discuss the fantasy, then discuss boundaries, limits and safewords, and have a post-event discussion. So naturally, you will be communicating more. By having to discuss hotwifing more increases communication, and because you are doing it together with your Queen, this deepens your connection.

Better Sex for Her

The quality of sex is going to determine the quality of your relationship. Let's face it, in normal long-term relationships, sex can get dull and repetitive. But hotwifing can dramatically change all of this because of the variety factor for her. You cannot achieve a completely new experience without changing locations and partners. It's not for everyone to make such dramatic sweeping changes to their sex lives, but interacting with new people can and does bring change to sex and relationships. How you navigate the changes is very important.

Hotwifing will introduce a sense of naughtiness and adventure to your life like you've never experienced before. Hotwifing can place the woman in charge and allows her to be the center of attention. For women who love being worshipped and adored, the idea of two men serving and watching her is thrilling in itself. The addition of new partners can help her to experience new positions, tips and tricks, techniques, and locations. Women need variety, and the more interesting and sexier the experience is, the more turned on the Queen gets.

Great Sex for Him

Men turned on by hotwifing have reported they cannot get the same arousal from anything else. Maybe it's the voyeurism, the competition sperm theory, the sight of the enjoyment on his Queen's face, or the thrill of watching what could be considered live porn. Men report major sexual arousal during hotwifing, and for him, he can either choose to watch or join in. He gets increased sexual pleasure and the assurance of a relationship that remains strong with his Queen.

Let's face it, 60 percent of men have engaged in infidelity, which means we cannot ignore men's need for variety and outside stimulation. Hotwifing achieves this but maintains trust and honesty while allowing the freedom to explore. Everything is perfect in relationships if any desire or activity doesn't hurt or negatively affect your partner. Contrary to popular beliefs, the desire to have sex with someone else doesn't always come out of mistrust and dissatisfaction, but instead it is brought about by trust and complete understanding of each other's needs, romantically and sexually. Any sexually active person who says that he or she can't think of anybody other than their sweetheart in bed or cannot fantasize about anyone might be lying. So, it is better to let someone experience something new to break the monotony built in your relationship.

Building of Trust

You build trust when you can share your deepest, darkest fantasies with someone who will not judge you for them but supports and helps you to experience them. Your Queen can't help but trust you when you are willing to allow her to explore and have the freedom to try new things and you both gain respect for each other for making the relationship or marriage a priority. When you ignore sexual issues in a relationship and you allow our sex life to grind to a halt, you do major damage that may never be able to be undone.

Hotwifing as a way to salvage a sex life is not the answer, but helps to enhance a sex life that requires some tweaking. The trust is built because you are not sneaking around, lying, or attempting to have outside affairs, while your partner remains unaware, in the dark, and ignored. The issue with cheating is the breaking of trust. Honesty in a relationship is more likely to keep a marriage or relationship together, and working on differences in sexual appetite, fantasies, and trying to spice things up can only lead to positive outcomes.

More Passion

When two people meet for the first time, they can develop passionate love which is a short-term, fiery, obsessive kind of feeling. In hotwifing, this can also happen because of the newness of it. Kinsey found the effects of passionate love on the brain is a person who is love-smitten and will often make choices that will seem illogical to others, such as prioritizing the object of their affection above work, friends, and family, no matter the trade-offs.

Studies using fMRI technology show when people fall in passionate love, the brain scan studies show that the maddening feelings of love are essentially a major mental-health crisis. The chemical storm of brain changes it causes are strikingly similar to drug addiction and obsessive-compulsive disorder. Love really does make us crazy. Therefore, couples can feel this euphoria in hotwifing, which leads to excitement, adventure, and more passion.

Experience shows that passionate love can be an addiction, and individuals in the early stage of intense romantic love show many symptoms of substance and non-substance or behavioral addictions, including euphoria, craving, tolerance, emotional and physical dependence, withdrawal, and relapse. This could explain why couples engaging in hotwifing seem to love doing it for extended periods despite it being controversial. eNot only are men experiencing tremendous feelings of love and respect for having such a desirable, beautiful Queen, but she experiences the attention and feelings of being desired, which can be very arousing for women. Hotwifing turns up the heat even more because the focus is on sex, and being sexy together also improves the connection between you and your Queen.

Chapter 9

Hotwifing and Desire

Hotwifing has a lot to do with desire. Male and female desire might not be as dissimilar as we've typically assumed. For decades, researchers promoted and believed that men have higher desires than women since significant studies confirm this finding. But more studies reveal that differences between the sexes may actually be closer than previously thought and skewed depending on how it was studied.

There is often the stereotype that men were with women who had a low desire for sex, but some studies have even found that women in relationships are as likely to be with a man who has lower desire. Others have found that women's desire changes according to the time of the menstrual cycle. During women's peak period of arousal, which occurs around ovulation, their sexual motivation is as strong as the men's.

Then there are the challenges of gender-related stereotypes about women being passive and not sexual. Women hold themselves back, deny their fantasies, give up on what they want, and sell themselves short on the idea that sex and love must be a certain way.

Women push themselves toward physical encounters they either do not want or have not allowed desire to adequately develop, thus, leading them to be in unfulfilling relationships. How science studies desire in women could be faulty because it's based on how men experience desire.

Even the variety of feelings during sex itself had gone unrecognized. Women do not necessarily experience the same progression of excitement, plateau, orgasm, and resolution that men do. Instead, the order can be shuffled. Sex itself can be the trigger for desire and arousal, or a first orgasm might lead to the desire for a second. For women, the desire may not come until they have orgasmed, which is why so many women become more sexually aggressive the more sex they may be having. What turns on one woman may not turn on another.

Today, modern women are exploring all options of pleasure which is why hotwifing has become so popular. I am witnessing more women over 50 and 60 showing themselves off as sexy and desirable in pictures in lingerie and bikinis on social media. Grandmothers in lingerie and thong bikinis, unheard of in the past, but are becoming the norm. Women are giving into their desire to be viewed as sexy goddesses, and hotwifing allows them to explore all that is pleasurable. Hotwifing is also more likely to be enjoyed once a woman starts doing it because the way desire works in women is they tend to become more sexually aroused once they are in sexy experiences.

Chapter 10

Hotwifing and Female Led Relationships

Since hotwifing is predominantly a female led activity today, many couples who are enjoying this lifestyle are already in a Female Led Relationship. An FLR is one where the woman takes the lead and assumes the role of the dominant partner, with men taking the more submissive role. The woman will be in charge of the important decisions and carries more authority in the relationship.

The Queen's decision must be respected and followed. The first rule of Female Led Relationships is that sex is for the Queen's pleasure. If you have come to an agreement that it is beneficial for her to interact with the Bull while you watch, then you must adhere to it. Perhaps the Queen decides she wants you to participate, and this is what you will do.

However, clear boundaries must be established for both of you and the outside man. Everything must be clearly explained to the Bull before engaging in anything to prevent unwanted activity. Maybe the Queen decides she wants to make the first move to start things off. In that case, this must be respected. Men in a Female Led Relationship must never take it upon themselves to initiate anything with hotwifing not authorized by the Queen. Since she will probably be the person engaging with a stranger, she needs to be careful and confident about how this is done. She needs to decide what she is comfortable with and what she would rather avoid.

Hotwifing should always be approached with great care and respect for all people involved. Consent is extremely important. In the Female Led Relationship, the man is the supportive gentleman. You are supporting the Queen's interaction with another man. As part of that support, if she decides she wants you to get involved, then you can do so. Hotwifing needs to be a positive experience for you and your Queen. The idea is that you are both in a Female Led Relationship and are in love. You both want to stay with each other in a long-term relationship.

The Queen successfully and ethically deals with having outside lovers and keeping her primary relationship strong. This is very challenging, so any decisions related to hotwifing must not be taken lightly. One way that you can show your true submission and devotion is in the preparation phase by helping her get ready for the event. Similar to a Queen preparing to attend an event, her helpers assist her in getting ready. When you spend some time assisting your Queen prepare, you reinforce your bond as her supportive gentleman.

Hotwifing can be an exciting part of a Female Led Relationship, because as the supportive gentleman, you are allowing your Queen to do what will make her happy. It can be a very exciting activity for both of you to do together, but you still need to follow the rules of FLR. Sex is for the Queen's pleasure first. You exist to bring the Queen pleasure. With your acceptance and respect throughout the interaction, you show your commitment to her happiness. This means you allow her to lead the interaction and obey her rules. You are respectful of her interaction with the outside man, the Bull, and you adhere to any agreements made. You encourage open communication before and after the act, ensuring you're both fulfilled by the experience.

CHAPTER 11

Is HotWifing the Same as Cuckolding?

Hotwifing and cuckolding are similar ways of expressing your sexuality as a couple while allowing your wife to have a good time. The main difference between Hotwifing and cuckolding is the humiliation aspect, as well as the man being generally submissive and ill-equipped for satisfying his Queen. For example, a cuckold is usually a man who enjoys being humiliated for being inadequate. He has a smaller penis and is unable to satisfy his woman. He may simply enjoy seeing another man with his woman.

In hotwifing, sometimes the dominant woman insists that she wants to have sex with a man, so it's much more of a female led activity. But hotwifing generally involves an alpha man who wants to show off his wife and derives pleasure from seeing other men desire her. He may even be adequate and get involved in the sex act, or he may allow his Queen to have the experience alone and hear the details afterward. The husband of a hotwife considers it a compliment to himself that other men desire his wife. He takes pride in having such a hot wife who is so sexually charged.

Hotwifing and cuckolding experiences are similar—a married woman engages in sexual relationships with other men with her man's consent. Often, these relationships are in pursuit of fulfilling the husband's or the couple's fantasies, and this can apply to any woman whose husband feels she is hot enough to attract another man for the cuckold; that he is not sexually capable of satisfying her alone. In the world of kinky sex, either form of expression means the husband desires some level of interaction between his wife and another man.

While the concept of another man holding, kissing, and making love to your wife is considered to be a bit abnormal, it is a fantasy that many men and women have. In fact, research has shown that a majority of men fantasize about watching their wives engage in some degree of sexual activity with another man. Today, many couples consider Hotwifing and cuckolding to be fun, exciting, and beneficial to their marriage. It is obvious why women like it as it allows them to fulfill their wildest sexual fantasies. In addition, many couples share this sexual fantasy of taking their relationship to a more kinky level.

Research shows that couples have fantasies about hotwifing, but many are afraid to express them to each other because they fear what their partner might think of them. So, one of the benefits of acting on a hotwifing fantasy is the real-life fulfillment of your most secret desire. It also provides a woman with a new-found modern freedom and the right for her to choose what she does with her body. Modern women do not want to be controlled by a man.

In female led marriage, women have the right to do as they see fit. The Queen gets the freedom to enjoy the company of the opposite sex. Many women in female led marriages enjoy the company of men other than their husbands. They practice the idea that modern women are not the property of their husbands. This modern way is allowing women to have the chance to enjoy life more. When a man allows his woman to be in the company of other men, she enjoys a refreshing kind of intimacy and freedom with all her men, including her husband.

In female led marriage, women are freed from the jealousy of their husbands. Jealousy is one of the major reasons many relationships fail. Jealousy arises from male ego concerns and male insecurities. This male ego-based jealousy is a contributing factor in many disagreements and breakups. As we discussed, jealousy comes from ancient genetic coding in men to protect their future lineage by making sure that his wife's offspring are his as well. Hotwifing is a modern experience that can help to rid the man of his feelings of jealousy. In a female led marriage, the wife can enjoy her freedom to be who she wants to be, she knows her husband will be obedient, and he will have her best interests and her pleasure at heart, which helps her trust him more and enjoy the marriage.

Relationships are built on trust and communication. Though counter-intuitive, hotwifing increases trust and communication within relationships. If you want to be really happy with a lasting relationship, you must ensure you understand and give each other the chance and freedom to be who you really are, including living out your most secret fantasies. Before you begin to dive into actual hotwifing, you both need to agree with each other that you want to do this. The women in Female Led Relationships are typically sexually dominant, while the man takes on a more submissive role, only becoming involved with her sexually or with her lover when the wife permits him to. Sometimes, the man will remain in chastity and completely celibate for the entire marriage.

As a man, you may feel that you have the hottest woman on earth, and every man desires to have a woman who is another man's dream. Hotwifing gives a man the perfect chance to allow other men to appreciate how beautiful and desirable his woman is, which typically serves to increase both his love and respect for her. It boosts both the man and the woman's confidence. In female led marriages and both hotwifing and cuckolding experiences, women have a chance to express themselves. When a woman knows that she has the support of her man to do whatever she desires, she feels great about herself, which helps to boost her own self-confidence. This type of open and honest relationship increases trust and communication between the couple and brings them closer together.

It is well known that Female Led Relationships increase intimacy. Hotwifing gives both the man and woman in a relationship the perfect chance to gain important knowledge about themselves and each other that can help raise their level of intimacy and connection. The new sexual adventures and the wide variety of options dramatically deepen a couple's bond. It provides a greater sense of sexual satisfaction for both husband and wife.

Hotwifing and cuckolding can create a lifestyle for attaining physical satisfaction. The woman can spend quality time with men who interest her, which quenches her thirst that would typically lead to affairs and betrayals in more traditional marriages, destroying trust and relationships. One of the main benefits of Female Led Relationships is that they stay together because they are far more open, honest, intimate, loving, and fulfilling than many people think.

CHAPTER 12

Is Hotwifing the Same as Polyamory?

Is hotwifing the same as polyamory? People often confuse hotwifing with polyamory, but they are different. A polyamorous relationship from the Greek word *poly* means "many," and Latin *amore* means "love" in a non-monogamous relationship. The couple can have intimacy with multiple partners all the time, and which is an actual lifestyle. These couples have the freedom to be non-monogamous, and there are still rules laid out that are followed.

A great example of this was in the movie *Savages*. All three characters lived together and each man had sex with the main female character "Ophelia" played by Blake Lively. Even the Mexican cartel characters criticized this type of living as "savage" compared to their way of killing and murdering associates. The irony is pervasive in this movie and serves as a good portrayal of modern polyamory. The three were considered the family unit.

Hotwifing is not the same. While the woman has sex with another man, he is not part of the main family unit and in general, hotwifing is not happening with a gay man or a transgender. Hotwifing is mainly about sex but does not involve living and inviting others into the family unit. I also believe that hotwifing appears to be much simpler as one night as opposed to navigating a relationship bond with three people. Hotwifing can be one or two nights of fun, whereas polyamory often involves living with multiple people on a day-to-day basis. These are two completely different scenarios and must not be confused.

One of the first Polyamorous groups was the Kerista communities that began in 1956 in New York and San Francisco by John Peltz Presmont, where a community was created to allow polyfidelity and swinging. The community promoted hippie principles of love and freedom. The idea that no one belonged to anyone. Anything goes. Good Vibes. Groups were arranged as Best Friend Identity Clusters made up of several men and women who rotated around sleeping with each other on a schedule. So, on any given night, each man would be sleeping with a different woman and vice versa. Polyfidelity offered a number of obvious advantages over more traditional family and intimacy styles. It caters to the desires of those who like sexual variety, yet allows this to occur in the context of lasting, deep, meaningful relationships.

This blend of spice and stability is very refreshing to people who, in other situations, have had to forfeit a stable home life in order to experience variety or vice versa. The problem of having unrealistic expectations of what one partner can provide that often occurs in two-adult families is solved; no one individual needs to be all things to anyone else. The Keristas were the first to use the word compersion which meant "free from jealousy." Happiness from another person's happiness." In the case of polyamory, compersion means happiness from seeing your partner happy in other relationships. Compersion can also occur in hotwifing, where the man has compersion from seeing his wife with another man for a night. Polyamory involves a living situation and deep relationship with multiple people, whereas hotwifing is merely a fun, short-term exploration.

CHAPTER 13

Why Does the Bull Like hotwifing?

What's in it for the extra man? The Bull. There are many men who love the idea of satisfying a Queen in front of her husband. In many ways, he is desired and is the center of attention of the Queen and the husband. There may be a bit of rivalry among suitors, and even though he is selected and approved by the husband, he gains confidence knowing he is the chosen one. He gets to engage in no-strings-attached sex with a hot married woman, which is much different than having sex with a single girl night after night.

Sometimes it's the thrill of being with an experienced, kinky couple as well as the fulfillment of the threesome or orgy fantasy. The outside man or Bull has the freedom to be with who he wants and walk away, with no jealous pushback or animosity. He's done a good deed, so feelings of accomplishment and success are also common. The Bull must be careful about falling in love or developing feelings for the Queen. The encounter will never result in a relationship, and he has to ensure he keeps this straight in his mind, no matter how many times he agrees to participate.

Some men develop fixations on the Queen because she is the strongest and most confident, powerful woman he has ever been with. Maybe she's older and more experienced and he's younger, and he begins to view her as a possible conquest or partner. Falling in love with the Queen would be disastrous for the Bull. He also needs to be cautious if he's in a relationship. Probably better not to engage with a hotwife with a significant other. Avoiding any chances of causing pain or hurt to a partner who is unaware of or likely to disapprove of the interaction is mandatory. The Bull or outside man should be single.

CHAPTER 14

How to Choose the Right Bull

The Bull is referred to the man your wife will engage with. You and your Queen will choose this Bull. He is the additional person who will be introduced into the hotwifing activity. His job is to satisfy your Queen, so great care will be needed when selecting the right man. Hygiene and safety must be at the top of the list. As difficult as it is to choose someone who is attractive and well-endowed, it will be important to insist on safety with all the precautions. While this can be a buzzkill, it might be wise to choose a man who takes great pride in his health and appearance.

The next challenge is to choose a man who is willing to join. The good news is that many men enjoy being asked to participate in hotwifing, and here are some of the reasons. Men have always had a deep fantasy about satisfying a woman's every need, and now, a single man who does not desire a relationship or marriage can get action without the deep commitment.

Sometimes these relationships become so deep that all three of you become friends, so in a way, the outside partner gets to be part of the sex but not have the constraints of the relationship. He is also satisfying the Queen, and in many ways, he is the star who has been brought into the relationship to spice it up. He may not necessarily be larger in size, but often he is more confident and able to satisfy the Queen. The position of a Bull is perfect for noncommittal men who want to have the titillating enjoyment of kinky sex without commitment.

Many couples get so carried away with the enjoyment of this fantasy that they rush into choosing an unsuitable man. One example is the best friend. This might seem logical since you know him and you probably both like him. However, a best friend is problematic for many reasons. First, he is emotionally connected, which means you both will continue to remain friends with him. Should the hotwifing fail to work out, you don't want the repercussions of harsh feelings and emotional ties. This can lead to complete destruction of the friendship, which can affect even your larger circle of friends.

Another example is to choose someone from your gym. This again may seem like a logical choice, especially from the health perspective, but unless you want to take the chance of not being able to return to your gym and talking about the experience with others there, then it is best to refrain from choosing a Bull in a familiar place.

Before you choose your Bull, it will be important to do some pre-screening of candidates and look for men in certain places. In the past, couples had no choice but to rely on Craigslist or swinging events.

Pre-Screening

One of the best ways to begin pre-screening is to use alternative dating sites and apps. Some popular ones are couplesdating.com, fetishhookups.com, localcuckolds.com, and fetlife.com. The advantage to this is that the man is already open to the idea and you and your Queen can meet with him anonymously with no real threat to your normal life.

Online dating has become a common part of life and seems like a logical and practical choice. There are several great lifestyle sites available now that allow for reviews and meet-up verifications from other local lifestyle couples. Having other people's stamp of approval is always a big plus because it suggests they have met that person offline before and would recommend him to others.

You can also read the Bull's online profile, take a look at their pictures, and get a feel for the type of person they are. For some couples, the Bull is strictly there for sex, and therefore you may feel like you don't need to know his whole life story, but making sure you are all in agreement with your expectations and boundaries when you do meet up, which can save a lot of hassle. You may also find that someone that initially looks good on screen isn't sexually compatible with your personality and tastes.

Don't be afraid to have an initial meeting for a drink or dinner to get comfortable and more familiar. Judging the chemistry is important, and you can't gauge this from online pictures. You can never tell if there will be chemistry in real life. This is why chatting with them for a bit beforehand can be worth your time and effort. Can they hold a normal conversation? Are they sexy? Is there an attraction? Do you feel safe?

Ideally, this meeting would involve both of you first, because even if you're going to be involved, you can provide your opinion. You may pick up on something about being a man that your Queen may have missed. It's also imperative that you both agree on the Bull that you do end up going with and the decision isn't a one-sided arrangement. Your Queen finding an attractive Bull is a requirement for moving forward, but other points must be addressed.

Of course, the same safeguards would apply. Meeting in a public place with someone who may have already expressed that he is interested.

First Meeting

One thing to consider is you and your Queen spending time choosing the man together, then you can go ahead first and meet him. The advantage of this is your participation is assured, and you can spend time ensuring that you are comfortable with the act, and you are confident about who will be with your wife. The next meeting can involve all three of you. This also ensures there are no awkward moments or negative feelings if the first meeting does not go well.

There is also a level of honesty and trust that you develop with the additional man. Therefore, ensuring that there is consent and open communication between everyone involved is crucial. Many couples skip this step, and men will allow their Queens to meet in private. This can cause feelings of being left out or ignored. While during cuckolding the feelings of humiliation are tied to being excluded and seen as the slave in the relationship, with hotwifing, it's important the husband also feels confident and derives his pleasure from watching and participating.

Meeting online can often be challenging, and there is always uncertainty with how much of a great fit the outside man or Bull will be. In this case, great care in the approach and first few meetings must be taken. On the other hand, since hotwifing is a female led activity, the Queen is generally in charge of the relationship, and what she decides, goes. If the

Queen meets the Bull and she has a less than positive experience, then she may decline to proceed.

At this time, you all abandon the hotwifing date until the Queen finds someone she likes and you are also in agreement. In this scenario, you must be 100 percent on board with allowing her to direct the interaction. This can be accomplished if you both are more experienced. If there is any hesitation from your Queen, you must abandon the idea and return to the discussion phase. How you both feel at every step of hotwifing is crucial.

Casual Meetups

Casual places to meet and talk before meeting up are swinging meetups and BDSM munch. A munch is when BDSM folks, or those who are merely interested in the lifestyle, join together away from play spaces to talk. While they can be held in just about any neutral territory, they most often take place in comfortable, public, accessible eateries.

They also commonly meet once a month, though in some places and branches of BDSM play more often than that. Munches also come in a variety of BDSM flavors, such as those focusing on general BDSM, and others that get much more specific, such as people into bondage, domination and/or submission, S&M, and other kinks. There is a lot of casual munch for hotwifing and swinging. It's important to remember that munches are not parties, but instead, are a way for kink folks to sit and chat. Don't try to be aggressive at these casual meetings and make sure to dress normally.

Generally, munches are light, social affairs, and while people can and do make meaningful connections with other people, don't treat them as only a place to cruise for partners.

Once you seem to have some chemistry with someone, only then can you take it to the next level of meeting privately.

These meetups can also educate and give you knowledge about hotwifing that you were unaware of. It's a great way to have a pleasant experience at your first munch and to view it as a learning experience. If you're new to the scene, say so and ask for people's advice and guidance. Kinky people love to teach new folks about what it means to be part of the community. Here, you can also learn more about parties, events, and clubs you can attend to meet a desired Bull.

Chapter 15

How to Turn Your Wife into a Hotwife

Hotwifing used to be a male led activity in which men convinced their wives or girlfriends to participate. Some women might be completely unaware of what hotwifing is all about. How do you get her interested? Studies indicate that Queens who are reluctant can be willing to at least discuss the subject if they are approached in the correct way.

And this could be the best starting point. It simply involves getting them used to the idea and talking through their concerns. Today, however, many women are leading and deciding how and with whom they will have sex, and sometimes, it could be with a man or a woman. Regardless of who the reluctant partner is, it is best to start slowly with these steps.

Start by Playing Adult Games

One of the easiest ways to begin to experience hotwifing and being sexy with an outsider is with adult games like playing strip poker in a club or party where there are also single men. Then slowly progress to some of the more explicit adult games that involve physical contacts.

If these kinds of adult games are played more often, this will allow the husband to get used to seeing his wife be naked before others, especially before other men. In fact, some men have used this type of experience to test their confidence and relationship. Other ideas are key parties where there is some light swapping or flirting. Or even swinging where the Queen is the main attraction.

Begin Discussions

Always begin all activities with a discussion. You and your Queen must set boundaries and limits and discuss your role in the act. This gives both of you some sense of security and confirms that your primary relationship or marriage is the priority. Nothing should ever be done to jeopardize this.

Your Queen needs to assure you that she is happy in the relationship. But if the marriage is shaky or there are any red flags or hesitation, then hotwifing may not be the best option. Most women do link sex with love, and new partners should be careful enough to avoid developing emotional attachment with the Bull. Keep things very fun and casual. Your Queen should not engage with the additional partner alone or in secret. Everything must be discussed openly with consent from all involved.

Introduce Fantasies

You can begin to introduce the subject of hotwifing to your Queen by discussing fantasies. The conversation should lead up to whether she would be excited to have sex with an outside partner while you were present or directly involved. Have her describe her ideal fantasy. What would it entail? Where would it happen? Who would be her ideal partner? Women often like to describe their fantasies with celebrities, but this is helpful, so you can begin to have an idea of whether she would be into it or not.

While it is not necessary to rush from this phase, use the time to ensure both of you get comfortable with the idea and how it would play out. Do you both agree to explore together? Maybe you both can research parties, events, conventions, or dating sites. Use the description of fantasies to be open and honest about how you would ideally proceed. Once you are confident your Queen is on board, you can proceed.

CHAPTER 16

What Are the Rules and Boundaries?

Couples engaging in hotwifing must have rules and boundaries that clearly define what occurs in the relationship and must be extended to include the Bull. One of the first rules to establish is where hotwifing will happen. Will it be at your house or the Bull's? Since your comfort and safety are important, having it in an environment you can handle is best. Some couples may choose a hotel room for complete anonymity. Not a bad choice. You can reserve it and invite the Bull over. Everyone is safe, and you are not entering private areas.

If this is not an option. You can choose your guest bedroom with no kids around. This way it's not in your private space. You can also choose your pool area, if the weather permits, as it's sexy and again allows you to keep your private areas private. The idea is that since this is a new adventure, keeping it separate from your day-to-day life is recommended.

When you have decided to do hotwifing, it is essential to set up clearly defined boundaries with you and your Queen first. How will it play out? Will your Queen approach the Bull or will both of you? Will the Queen decide how it will play out by giving you instructions, or will you be participating right from the start? This is where a Female Led Relationship is so beneficial because the woman makes the rules.

She decides on what will happen and all you need to do is follow. So, boundaries must also involve what happens if anyone becomes uncomfortable or wants to stop. It should be clearly established that you abort immediately. Getting into arguments of jealous fits of rage should never occur. Doing so keeps everything running smoothly. Maybe your Queen wants to stop. The appropriate and respectful response is to all agree. The Bull's state of mind must also be considered, and if he is unable to perform, you decide a respectful way to stop. At no time should anyone be made to feel pathetic or bad. You want to prevent any chance of a fun situation spiraling out of control.

Another important point in boundaries is to discuss the importance of honesty. The bond between you and your woman must be maintained, and at no time should either of you engage with the Bull alone or without consent. The idea of hotwifing, as opposed to cheating, is the lying, hiding, and secrecy that often occurs with infidelity. Maintaining trust is the biggest factor. I noticed that often in cheating it is the dishonesty that often does the most destruction to relationships, which is why trust and the understanding that both people will always be honest and open about hotwifing is the key. It should be understood that there will be no emotional ties with the Bull from either of you.

These Are Some of the Steps to Begin

The best place to start is with open communication. Discuss everything very openly. What do you like, and what does she like? How do you see the activity unfolding? What are things that are completely forbidden? Which things would you be open to exploring?

The next step is to spend some time talking about the fantasy and explore anything uncomfortable about it. Communication about everything is going to make things so much smoother. Decide on safe words on what to do if there is anything that should feel strange.

Then it's time to go out and engage with people. Spend some time talking about it or hanging out with others in a bar setting. Without directly engaging a single man, you could set up scenarios to approach a single man in a bar to just gain experience of being comfortable talking with a third. Perhaps your Queen wants to dance with another man and flirt with him while you watch. This can be an easy way to determine how you both feel about it.

One of my first experiences with this was when one of my ex-boyfriends encouraged me to dance with a friend of his. At first, I was a bit shocked that he did not care, and I was extremely uncomfortable with the fact that he was being very aggressive coming onto me in front of my boyfriend who had no issue with it. I later learned that it was something he liked, and he and his friend were used to it. Needless to say, the relationship broke up, but what I learned was that merely dancing and flirting in a scenario like this is enough to determine if hotwifing will be right for you.

If you both cannot get past this step or there are signs of jealousy, you may not be ready. It is important to get comfortable with the process and be okay if the first time does not go well. After each encounter, even at a bar, discuss your feelings about it openly. Discuss any hesitations and any areas to improve. Maybe you did not like how you felt excluded when she positioned herself with a third. Or you liked that she took the initiative to approach a man and then invited both of you to sit and chat. It is important to discuss everything and decide if hotwifing is worth pursuing. I can recall one of my ex-boyfriends asking me to be in an open relationship and me saying that I was fine with it, when in reality, I was not ready to pursue anything at the time. I think it was my unwillingness to be honest that eventually drove a rift between us.

The next step is to go online. Lots of dating sites are already set up for hotwifing, with many mainstream ones having options to explore this activity. Spend time reading and looking at profiles and deciding together a suitable Bull. Be respectful when you first approach someone and make the initial dates a time to meet and talk. The more comfortable you are with the Bull, the better it will be. Keep personal details to a minimum and always make sure everyone is on board with safety and precautions.

Create some general rules for the night. For example, you may say to your partner, "Tonight let's go out with Dan to dinner and afterwards we can come back, go in the hot tub, and just start there." Nothing has to happen. It can just be a night of getting to know him and having fun.

Later on, as you get more comfortable you can have some hot times in a hot tub with just kissing or allowing the Bull to feel her up. The Queen's decision about how far she is willing to go must be established, but there is no harm in starting with baby steps. The more smoothly each encounter goes, the better it is. Some couples progress with just fingering or use of sex toys only as the exploration continues. Then once everyone is on board, you can all plan for the full experience of the Bull having intercourse with your woman while you watch.

Some variations that can be done before intercourse is having oral sex with your woman, then let her be fucked by the Bull. Whatever happens, she must make the rules and you can decide if you agree. It's much more fun and inclusive for you to participate in some way, with the main act reserved for the woman and the Bull.

You should never feel ashamed if you are feeling jealous. Jealousy is a powerful human emotion. It doesn't mean you're closed-minded or prudish. No matter how "cool" you are, jealousy is going to flare up. That doesn't mean this kind of relationship isn't for you. Jealousy typically means you need some special attention. As partners in a significant relationship with someone, you must be willing to work through feelings.

Opening up yourselves to new sexual experiences can bring on all sorts of feelings, and you must be allowed to experience them openly. Many couples go through this, and it is perfectly normal. The emotions of jealousy, passion, and desire are all part of the thrill ride, which makes this so exciting to everyone involved. You both also need to be respectful of the Bull and if there are any hesitations.

CHAPTER 17

Types of Hotwifing Solo Hotwife

A solo hotwife does all hotwifing adventures alone. This can extend into the more modern female led swinging where the Queen decides she will only do hotwifing alone. Some hotwives only play when their husband is also present, so these couples only do threesomes, wife swapping, or the husband may just like to watch.

Other hotwives prefer to go to clubs and bars alone to hook up while their husbands remain at home.

There are two reasons for a setup like this. The first is the couple share a kink where they both get off on her going out solo to have sex with someone else, him consenting to it and being excited by it, and when she comes home to tell him all about it, and he is turned on by her descriptions they may have some playtime of their own.

The second reason is that they have more of an open relationship. They are both secure enough in their relationship and respect each other's sexual desires and needs. They encourage each other to explore them with other people. The Bull can engage freely with the Queen without bringing up or asking questions about the husband. In this way, the Bull can approach the situation as a normal sexual interaction with a woman. It's easier as it only involves two people.

Vixen and Stag

A Vixen and Stag couple is one of the most common types of hotwifing. The Vixen is the woman, and the Stag is the male in the relationship. He is not submissive and considers himself an alpha male. He controls the entire situation, including the extra man. Single men who want to be a buck for a Stag and Vixen threesome, accept that their position to the couple will always come below the Stag, regardless of whether playing in a threesome or solo with the Vixen. The buck is always considered secondary in this interaction even as the Queen is interacting with him. The Stag will generally attempt to be the director or control the interaction, though today in FLR hotwifing, the Queen is in charge and the Stag is second.

The difference between the Stag and Vixen is that this is not a cuckolding scenario where the husband is purposely made to feel shame or forced to be submissive. Many Queens who have alpha husbands enjoy this form of hotwifing because the man maintains his alpha personality while having his sexual fantasies fulfilled. The Stag can also choose to join in, and he will participate in an alpha position, instead of simply being cast aside and forced to be humiliated.

It is important to make these distinctions clear to the extra man so that he knows if he is acting as the buck, secondary to the Stag, or he is the Bull in a cuckolding scenario. For couples, it is important to ensure you are both aware of what type of fantasy you are fulfilling to avoid any misunderstanding or breaking of agreements.

The female led hotwifing version of this scenario means a husband has no choice but to end up sharing his wife to avoid losing her. It often happens in couples where the wife is extremely hot with an average hubby, or where the hubby struggles over time to make her happy sexually, which leads to frustration and her looking for an extra cock. In the more extreme case, the wife has or has considered finding extra relationships while a hotwife lifestyle can keep the couple together and the wife happy.

Most wives still love their husbands and are not really into having other relationships, especially if they have a family. Yet they are hot, beautiful, and have a high sex drive which makes them very unsatisfied. In this scenario, the Queen will demand having a Bull, and the husband can watch or join in at her direction. The Bull must be careful to listen and understand what the Queen's needs are without saying any derogatory comments or making the husband feel inadequate or ignored. It's a real balancing act.

Submissive Hotwife

Originally, the normal hotwife would be coerced into the lifestyle purely for the dominant man's voyeurism. The woman has no power in this interaction. The husband or boyfriend would be directing the activities and orders her to have sex as he enjoys. This can include tying her up for surprise sex with a man or letting a bunch of guys uses and abuse her in a gangbang as he watches. In the movie 9 ½ *Weeks*, Mickey Rourke's character arranges a hotwifing scene and forces Kim Bassinger's character to engage in sex while blindfolded with another man. This experience was so traumatizing to her that it was the beginning of the end of their relationship.

In this type of hotwifing lifestyle, the couple may already enjoy some sort of BDSM sex life. This is not considered the modern form of hotwifing, and most women will not feel empowered or enthusiastically engage in this form. This type of hotwifing also borders on non-consensual and is very dangerous in today's climate of the Me Too movement and sexual harassment.

Bulls must make sure to communicate with both the Queen and the husband in organizing the event. He will need reassurance that you understand your role and his needs too. Ultimately you are still in a situation where the wife needs more, and your role is to deliver that. However, you must be more careful in pleasing them as a couple instead of just taking care of the wife's needs.

Queen of Spades

Queen of Spades is nearly identical to the cuckoldress, except that the woman will only sleep with black men. In cuckolding lifestyle, there is a huge focus on black men on the internet, especially their big black cocks (BBC). Obviously, this creates a special type of hotwife who only sleeps with black men, and the only white cock she may get is her husband's. Her husband can still maintain an alpha role as an observer or some may be allowed to engage. Bulls must be careful to not overstep boundaries or make derogatory comments or racial slurs about the husband. This is still a situation of three people engaging together even if the husband is not actively involved.

Slutwife

This hotwife is promiscuous by choice and easy. She has sex easily and cannot get enough of extra male attention. She'll have sex in cars, parking lots, bars, parties, offices, and sex clubs. This is another variant of the standard hotwife relationship in which there are agreements on what can and cannot be done and who the Queen will engage with.

The slutwife relationship dynamic is based on her continuing a slut lifestyle of having sex with any man or woman she desires. She still has sex with the Stag, her husband, or main partner; however, he doesn't get to have a say in who she flirts and has sex with. Alternatively, in some slutwife relationships, the woman is not even required to tell the Stag who she slept with. This form of hotwife follows much more the rules of an open relationship. Sometimes it is her husband or boyfriend who encourages her to sleep with more men.

On the other hand, it can happen at the beginning of the relationship as she puts this as a ground rule for him to accept. That she already has a slut life, and he must accept it to start the relationship or to marry her. If he is into this kink, both will be fortunate, and they will have lots of adventures. This lifestyle can extend into cuckolding, where everyone knows that the man lets his wife or girlfriend sleep with others. And also, they may have group sex parties, gangbang parties, and she will experience multiple Bulls to have double penetration.

Swinging/Wife Swapping

Swinging is generally couples having fun with other couples. Swinging will tend to happen at parties, clubs, or events. Couples will interact with other couples, and they will often swap spouses for sexy fun. They may also practice group sex, and this can become a regular occurrence between some couples, and as a result, they sometimes develop trust and bonds, and everyone's sex life is improved as a result considering it offers some variety. Some hotwives like to play the part of a single unicorn, an unattached single lady who joins in with swinging couples while her husband watches. Hotwifing can begin with attending swinging parties, where a couple may go and watch for pleasure and decide to participate later on.

Chapter 18

The First Hotwifing Encounter

Once all the discussion, practice, and agreement have happened, it's now time to experience your first encounter. This is likely to have lots of excitement and anticipation.

The first thing you'll want to do is ensure you are equipped with your safety items, for example, condoms, birth control, and lube. Have extra towels, tissues, sheets, toys, and outfits readily available. You may want to reserve a hotel room or a place separate from your main home. If you have kids, you'll want to ensure they are not exposed in any way to this activity. It's best to set schedules and choose a time to meet. It may be a good idea to meet at a restaurant or bar, then go to a hotel. You should both try to dress to impress in something that is applicable to the act. If your Queen wants to bring extra outfits or sex toys, she can pack these things. Personal hygiene is of the utmost importance, which is why a hotel room works since you'll have access to a bathroom.

If you decide to have it in your home, it might be wise to designate a specific room, so you can set it up with the mood and ambiance of your choosing. Pools, hot tubs, Jacuzzis, beachfront with access to a beach, or a penthouse suite overlooking the city are all wonderful areas to reserve for the initial encounter.

Start with getting everyone comfortable. Have some drinks, listen to music, and talk. You can begin with some light play with your Queen and watch her getting undressed or engaging in light foreplay with the extra man. Just engage slowly and sexy to get everyone in the mood. Then you can all move to the bedroom. If your Queen has decided you will watch, go to your chair and allow her to lead. Keep an open mind and enjoy the experience with no judgments.

She should already have determined how she wants to have intercourse and allow things to unfold. Be open and stick to your established boundaries. No one should go off-script.

It may be wise to make the first encounter short. Be aware of how you feel during the first time to decide if it will happen in the future. The key is to enjoy the moment. Focus on your Queen and her enjoyment. Refrain from intervening unless she specifically allows you to jump in. Then only focus your attention on her. The more comfortable everyone is, the better things will flow.

Some couples will have a safeword, where she beckons you to switch. Maybe she needs a break and wants to engage in some light touching with you. The safe word can be anything you want. Some examples are "switch," "tap out," or "time." Ensure you discuss it with the Bull/Buck so that he understands the boundaries. If there is no oral sex, let him know. It's best to avoid any surprises at the beginning where it can escalate into a disagreement.

Once the encounter is done, the Bull can leave, and you and your Queen can continue together, cuddle, or talk. Take showers or just unwind. It is important to have a period of togetherness after the act.

Karen and Thomas's Hotwifing Experience

Karen, 40, and Thomas, 45, agreed to share their experience with me. Karen describes, "We were first introduced to hotwifing through friends who had been in the lifestyle for many years. Over drinks one night, they described to us in detail how they found the Bull, met with him, and continued to have sex with him for many months. They were so enthusiastic and happy about the experience we knew we had to try it. We were your average couple, two kids, both corporate executives with busy demanding lives. We tried everything to make the sex more interesting, but we were still madly in love with each other.

"At first, we had no idea what to do. We tried to use Tinder to meet men, but as soon as I mentioned I was married, they were turned off. Then we used specialized sites and parties where people were into exploration. We met our Bull Mark online. He was sweet, 26, no desire for a relationship. He met us at a bar, we talked, laughed and at one point he stroked my thigh while maintaining eye contact with me and my husband. For me, it was near orgasmic, and my husband was turned on as well. Mark knew how to flirt, and he was very manly. He took his cues from Thomas, which made it even more exciting for me to have two men obsessed with me.

"When we were going to have our first encounter, we went to a hotel. We booked the room, and Mark just came up. It was thrilling. Thomas dressed me in lingerie he picked out like I was getting ready for a ball. It was very intimate, and I could see how much he cared about me and this whole experience. Mark arrived, took a shower, and came out in his towel. Thomas was happy sitting and watching. Mark was nice to start with light touching and massage, and he kept his towel on, so he could act like a massage therapist giving a massage. It helped to ease into it. He massaged me and then dropped his towel, and I thought I was going to explode right there.

"The sight of his hard, toned body on top of me, throwing me around, but being respectful to Thomas. Thomas enjoyed shouting instructions, and Mark obeyed and did what my husband commanded. In this way, he was participating. We did so many different positions as Mark was strong enough to help me to try getting fucked against the wall, against the window, in a chair, and more. I think the one thing I realized was that it never reduced the love or bond I had with Thomas, and he enjoyed being the executive and director that he was in life. He enjoyed giving the commands, and I enjoyed the variety. When it was all done, Mark took a shower and left, so Thomas and I were free to cuddle and talk. He was like a kid in a candy store. He was excited, happy, laughing, and relaxed. I was the same. We bonded more because we both felt like our sexual fantasies had been fulfilled."

Chapter 19

Creating Perfect Hotwifing Scenarios

Now that you have successfully accomplished your first encounter, this chapter will reveal how to keep creating perfect hotwifing scenarios. Here are a few suggestions.

Attend Formal Fetish Parties

One of my most memorable times was getting invited to a party straight out of the movie *Eyes Wide Shut*, complete with mansion, costumes, and passwords. It was unbelievable. The advantage is that you meet people in the same lifestyle and may be open to join you on your hotwifing adventure. This can spice up your relationship with new ideas and help you to find more than one suitable Bull. These parties often come with their own firm rules and opportunities to explore.

Add Costumes

There is a reason we love Halloween and people love dressing up. Wearing costumes during sex is no different.

They allow you to be someone else, enhancing the fantasy. You and your Queen can dress up, or you can watch while she and the Bull use costumes. It is important to keep sexiness alive. At a minimum, your Queen should be in sexy lingerie. Refrain from wearing normal underwear such as you in "tighty whities" and she in granny panties.

I have had to suggest to many couples the importance of keeping it sexy. Yes, you want to be comfortable, but sweatpants and sweatshirts don't cut it when you are trying to have an adventure. You as a doctor and she as a nurse with the Bull as the patient is so much more exciting. Costumes are great for those involved and add lots of variety. Costumes also help to distinguish between fun encounters and love-making sessions with your Queen.

Change Up the Locations

Change your locations. Maybe you meet at a club, dance, flirt, then hit the hot tub or maybe have dinner before going to a hotel room. Las Vegas has so many options for sexy hotels to put you in the mood. Los Angeles and NYC also offer several options. Plus, you can be assured that everyone there is interested in variety. Toronto's Drake hotel offers a sex menu. Keep the fantasy alive with lots of variety.

Set Up a Playroom

Who can forget the sumptuous playroom in *Fifty Shades of Grey* Christian Grey knows how to create the perfect playroom with luxurious red carpeting and high-quality leather furniture. Many couples have created similar playrooms which are kept locked and private as Mommy and Daddy's special room. The advantage is that it is private and can be filled with all sorts of adult toys to use with your Bull.

Many couples have added swings, sex cushions, and BDSM crosses with whips to add some light bondage to the experience. The idea is to make it as fun and fantastical as possible.

Be Spontaneous

Maybe you are out at a party, bar, or on vacation. Be spontaneous. You could strike up a conversation, do some flirting, go to a sexy after-hours spot, or a strip club. Sometimes being spontaneous and naughty can lead to some thrilling moments. Check out a sex club randomly one night. Just opening your mind can lead to some exciting hotwifing adventures.

Go On an Adult Vacation

One of the best ways to do hotwifing is to go on adult vacations. Today there are a number of these resorts that are set up specifically for adventurous couples looking for exploration. Resorts like Desire, Maya Riviera in Mexico, and The Ranch in Las Vegas are some places that can provide this type of experience. The advantage of the resort is that it's anonymous, but most people there are in the lifestyle.

Chapter 20

How to Deal with Hesitations

There may be a situation where you or your Queen have hesitations about hotwifing. Many men don't always feel confident about allowing their woman to engage with another man, and there is the fear that she will be stolen away and become obsessed with the Bull. This was the reason to refrain from engaging with a friend or someone with an emotional connection.

In a Female Led Relationship, the Queen makes the decision and you must follow her rules. However, you and your Queen should come to an understanding about how hotwifing will enrich your current relationship and assess the reasons for adding it to your life.

However, sometimes the Queen is new to the lifestyle, and it is the man who must try to introduce it to her. There will be normal hesitations about it, so you should begin by introducing the idea as a way to spice things up and have some adventure. You can explain that you will enjoy voyeurism and explore it safely. Explain that this is for her pleasure and her happiness is your priority.

Many modern women will be open as it naturally benefits them. Who doesn't want an attractive man worshipping you once in a while? Some women now have a voracious appetite for sex and can feel happy that her needs are being satisfied. I can recall the countless nights when I felt empty and unsatisfied with the sex and longed for more. But my upbringing and religious conditioning forbid me to explore these alternatives. You can assure your Queen that it's not shameful or wrong, as long as you both can reach an agreement. It's perfectly okay for a woman to explore her sexuality with the body that she owns and controls. It is outdated for men to think that they own a woman's body.

The most important point is to communicate and talk about it at length before beginning. Start fantasizing about it together and think about how you both would want it to unfold and get turned on. You can get her to start by imagining that the other man is there during sex at first. If it turns both of you on, then you can figure out if it's right for you.

Just talking about it will be a huge turn-on for both of you. Describing how it might happen and what would occur is a great initial way to open up about it. Discussing fantasies together can add to the excitement by foreshadowing what is about to happen and formulating the perfect scenario. Go out and start immersing her in the possibilities of this type of relationship. Talk, flirt, dance, and get her accustomed to places open to alternative lifestyles. There are several fetish clubs around where you both can meet people in the lifestyle. The most important thing to do with your woman is to assure her that you are still 100 percent committed to her. Make a promise that whatever you do with hotwifing will be done together and you will be attentive to her needs.

Spend time asking what she likes. When my partner was interested in my fantasies and what turned me on, I was shy at first to talk about it, but once I began to get comfortable, the flood gates opened. All I wanted to do was try new things. You get hooked. Women who are generally much more conservative in their experiences can begin to open up and have fun.

What has to be emphasized is that hotwifing and any other alternative lifestyle activity should be something you always do together. Your Queen is not expected to go out and do this on her own. Nor should she. Hotwifing should be approached as the extra activity you do together.

Other hesitations may include her not wanting to do certain things. Your Queen may be all excited to go on your first hotwifing fate, but she begins to hesitate at the time of the act. It is of the utmost importance to meet with the Bull to discuss everything before planning the first date. Not only will there be time to get comfortable, but you can discuss all limits.

Once you are in the act, if there are hesitations, be sure to feel comfortable about stopping and allowing her to deal with her feelings at the moment. If anyone has strong feelings about proceeding, abort the date. There should be an unwritten rule that it's okay to stop. Set these guidelines early on and be respectful. Hesitations should never be ignored or mocked. The most important rule to follow is comfort, acceptance, and consent.

Chapter 21

Avoid Common Pitfalls

As with anything new worth exploring, hotwifing can have some pitfalls that you and your Queen will need to avoid. During Lehmiller's interview with CNN, he states, "We found several personality factors that predict more positive experiences acting on hotwifing fantasies. For those who have a lot of relationship anxiety or abandonment issues, who lack intimacy and communication, and who aren't careful, detail-oriented planners, acting on a consensual non-monogamy fantasy could very well be a negative experience."

Another common pitfall is inviting a friend or relative to join in during hotwifing. Let's face it, we are human, and we love our friends. Quite often, couples can place a great deal of trust in a friend or relative. We figure that if we engage with people, we know it may be easier and you'd have lots of fun. But here is the downside. Details of your adventure slip out at the wrong time, like at a party or family dinner. Any issues relating to the event can never be avoided and could lead to the demise of the friendship. In addition, forming emotional ties can easily happen with people you know personally, so it is best not to engage in hotwifing with close friends or relatives.

Another pitfall is to get carried away with the fantasy that you both neglect the primary relationship. After your hotwifing encounter, it is extremely important to share the experience with your Queen and discuss things you each liked about it and disliked. You both also need to spend some time together having intimate times and sex. Some couples reconnect with oral sex or lovemaking worship sessions. This is crucial to keep the bond and the strength of the main relationship alive. It helps to ensure you both feel connected in your primary relationship. It helps to keep hotwifing as the side adventure you have from time to time. At no point should you or your partner form an emotional bond with the Bull. He is not part of the primary relationship.

When Hotwifing Is Not Advisable?

Hotwifing is not for couples who struggle with jealousy issues. Jealousy is one of the leading causes of failed relationships regardless of swinging lifestyle status. Some women struggle with jealous husbands who can't handle when another man looks their way, which often causes bitterness and resentment. Trying to placate a jealous husband while hotwifing leads some women to stifle their sexuality in an attempt to attract less attention. If you can't be celebrated for who you are, you can't be your best self in a relationship.

Psychologist, Lisa Firestone says, "When it comes to their intimate relationships, couples can make any decision they want about monogamy, as long as this decision is mutually agreed upon by both partners." Emotional risk is something else to consider. Even if you're completely on board at the start, feelings can change at any time. One person may decide they want to stop, the Bull may begin to experience more jealousy than he bargained for, or one or both people hooking up could become too attached. Hotwifing requires complete honesty from everyone involved every step of the way. Communicate frequently to make sure you're all still on the same page. If anyone is uncomfortable or unsure, or if anything feels off, stop and figure out what to do next.

For any relationship to work, there are certain fundamental qualities to be aware of. In an open relationship, in which a couple chooses not to hide or allow infidelity, it is all the more important to encourage honest communication and healthy ways of handling emotions like jealousy, victimization, or a desire to control.

Some of the elements you'll want to avoid if you want to keep things close, consistent, and exciting between you and your partner include dishonesty and fear. Irreparable damage is done when there is dishonesty in a relationship and it is finally discovered. Lying leads to pain that cannot be undone.

Dr. Firestone cites research that shows unfaithful individuals are less likely to practice safe sex than people in open relationships. This act of deception thus poses both a physical and emotional threat to their partner. "Whatever their decision is regarding monogamy, if two people want their relationship to stay strong, they must strive to be open and truthful and to ensure their actions always match their words." An open relationship without honesty is disastrous and deception is likely to lead to the same feelings of hurt and distrust. We may not be able to control our attractions, but we can control how we behave and how we deal with these feelings. Being open with your partner and encouraging openness will inspire an atmosphere of honesty.

Fear is another major issue. Fear of intimacy and fear of losing your partner as a result of hotwifing. Fear is a tremendous problem because it can make us paralyzed in a relationship. Couples find it difficult to get past the feeling that they could lose one another and grow apart. Maybe you think your Queen will get swept away by the Bull, so you begin to have and harbor these fears. What makes this even more complicated is that this fear can sit below the surface, so it isn't entirely conscious. Instead of thinking, "I'm scared of losing her," we will have thoughts like, "She is too good for me. I can't make this kind of commitment right now. I don't want to get hurt when she leaves."

Fear can leave a lasting destructive imprint on what could have been a fun activity, so it is important to get it out in the open and discuss it openly. Reassuring each other through this process is vital. If you're interested in hotwifing or an open relationship, you may want to determine why. Are you interested in sexual freedom only? Or is there something missing from your current relationship and you're just moving away from your partner? No matter what type of relationship you are in, when engaging in hotwifing, you'll have to get to know and challenge your own fears. These fears often come from old feelings of hurt, rejection, or loss. It is beneficial to deal with the underlying reasons for wanting to do this so that it is clear you both are doing it for the right reasons.

CHAPTER 22

Practicing Safe Sex

Ensuring safe sex at all times is extremely important during hotwifing. There is nothing worse than your partner, you, or the Bull ending up with an STD (sexually transmitted disease). STDs are sexually transmitted diseases. This means they are most often—but not exclusively—spread by sexual intercourse. HIV, chlamydia, genital herpes, genital warts, gonorrhea, some forms of hepatitis, syphilis, and trichomoniasis are STD.

It goes without saying that no encounter should ever involve the omission of a condom and other safeguards. Using a condom correctly every time you have sex can help you avoid STDs. Condoms lessen the risk of infection for all STDs. The failure of condoms to protect against STD/HIV transmission usually results from inconsistent or incorrect use rather than product failure.

- Inconsistent or nonuse can lead to STD acquisition because transmission can occur with a single-sex act with an infected partner.

- Incorrect *use* diminishes the protective effect of condoms by leading to condom breakage, slippage, or leakage. Incorrect use more commonly entails a failure to use condoms throughout the entire sex act, from start of sexual contact to finish, after ejaculation.

These are some suggestions to ensure proper use:

- Use a new condom for every act of vaginal, anal, and oral sex throughout the entire sex act (from start to finish). Before any genital contact, put the condom on the tip of the erect penis with the rolled side out.
- If the condom does not have a reservoir tip, pinch the tip enough to leave a half-inch space for semen to collect. Holding the tip, unroll the condom all the way to the base of the erect penis.
- After ejaculation and before the penis gets soft, grip the rim of the condom and carefully withdraw. Then gently pull the condom off the penis, making sure that semen doesn't spill out.
- Wrap the condom in a tissue and throw it in the trash where others won't handle it.
- If you feel the condom break at any point during sexual activity, stop immediately, withdraw, remove the broken condom, and put on a new condom.
- Ensure that adequate lubrication is used during vaginal and anal sex, which might require water-based lubricants. Oil-based lubricants (e.g., petroleum jelly, shortening, mineral oil, massage oils, body lotions, and cooking oil) should not be used because they can weaken latex, causing breakage.

You both may want to get tested so that you can offer evidence of clean and healthy. You may want to request this of the Bull as well, so everyone feels safe. It may also be warranted to have a discussion of exclusivity with the Bull. Maybe it can be decided that if he is having sex with your wife, he reserves himself at least for that time period to only be with you both. This may introduce pressure and a bit of buzzkill, but if safety is your major concern, it cannot be avoided. Your Queen will need to ensure that she is also protected against pregnancy. It is interesting how in the past, hotwifing was criticized for the fact that it involved an adulterous man who would often be baring another man's child. Today, modern hotwifing does not have to be an unpleasant consequence, especially if the right safeguards are taken.

Chapter 23

How to Deal with Disagreements

It is perfectly normal to have disagreements when exploring Hotwifing and other types of alternative relationships. You and your Queen may experience jealousy, or you may disagree on how the Hotwifing experience may unfold. You may not want her to perform certain acts or on how many times it should be done.

The first thing to realize is that disagreements are normal, and it is best to discuss them in an open fashion. After each encounter, one suggestion is to discuss what happened and what should not happen. During these sessions, it's important to be honest about feelings. If there was jealousy, get it out in the open and decide whether you should continue or not.

There may be times where you may not have agreed with what the Bull did. Again, open conversation with your Queen and the Bull is needed and should not be underestimated. In general, the Queen makes the decisions on how and what should be done, so you will want to allow her to be in charge. This takes the pressure off you and allows you to enjoy the experience. Try to refrain from being too critical but review the rules and boundaries. The idea is that hotwifing is just an activity you add to your life; it is not your entire life and should be treated as such.

Here are some key areas to discuss:

- Are you enjoying the sexual experiences?
- Are you interested in exploring together or alone?
- What other kinds of sexual fantasies can we explore?
- What kinds of sexual fantasies are off-limits?
- Is there a "line" that you do not want me to cross?
- What is your dream of the perfect hotwifing experience?
- Is there anything we should not do in hotwifing?
- How do you feel emotionally?
- Do you feel any jealousy?
- How many times is it healthy to do hotwifing a month?
- Should we remain friends with the Bull?
- What do we do when it's time to move on?
- What happens if we are not in agreement about this lifestyle?
- How do we handle our kids?
- How often should we talk about things?
- Should I be more submissive?
- Should you be more demanding?

Our early experiences in relationships, starting with the ones we had with our parents or primary caretakers, heavily influence the psychological defenses we form and often face throughout our lives. These defenses may have been strategies we adopted to survive less than ideal conditions in our childhood. These adaptations may have helped us as kids, but they can continue to hurt us in our adult relationships.

Oftentimes, when we first fall in love, we are in an undefended state in which we are more open to another person. However, as we get closer, we may experience fears around intimacy and revert to old defenses. We may become more critical and guarded or become more anxious and controlling depending on our defense system. In addition, we may even be attracted to people who are likely to hurt us in the very same ways we were hurt as children. So, you and your Queen are dealing with all of this while exploring this new lifestyle.

One thing you will learn in an open relationship is to listen to what your partner says, even if it is challenging or frightening. You will learn to accept discomfort and go with it. Nobody said this was going to be the path of least resistance, in fact, it is challenging, but it is also very rewarding. This approach will not necessarily protect you from being hurt. We often feel fireworks with people whose defenses fit ours and who reaffirm old, familiar, often unpleasant ways of feeling about ourselves and others. While we may feel passion and excitement in the initial stages of these relationships, our defenses will often eventually get in the way, as we find ourselves either becoming more and more distant or increasingly pursuing our partner in ways that trigger their own defense system.

There are certain things that need to happen for an open relationship to be a healthy and happy experience. I believe there are essential things that must be done in any relationship.

Dr. Lisa Firestone, a psychologist, found that "some essential characteristics that fit the description of a loving relationship include expressions of affection, both physical and emotional, a wish to offer pleasure and satisfaction to another, tenderness, compassion, and sensitivity to the needs of the other, a desire for shared activities and pursuits, an appropriate level of sharing of one's possessions, an ongoing, honest exchange of personal feelings and the process of offering concern, comfort, and outward assistance for the loved one's aspirations." If you and your Queen commit to these as principles, you both will be much more likely to stay in touch with your loving feelings and keep the passion, attraction, respect, and admiration as living forces in your relationship.

You need to be extremely honest about feelings of jealousy. Jealousy is a natural human emotion. Yet, the way we use it can be very destructive. Dr. Firestone states, "Lurking behind the paranoia toward our partners or the criticisms toward a perceived third-party threat are often critical thoughts toward ourselves. She finds that a person's "critical inner voice" can bombard his or her mind with harmful suspicions and accusations that fuel feelings of jealousy. She often finds that what people are telling themselves about what's going on with their partner is usually worse than what is actually going on. It is important to discuss it openly with your Queen.

If you are scared, worried, angry, or upset, say it. Disagreements erupt when there is a perceived feeling of distrust. Even when our worst fears materialize and we learn of a partner's affair, we frequently react by directing anger at ourselves for being "foolish, unlovable, ruined, or unwanted." These shaming attitudes toward ourselves and our partners can breed an environment of distrust. If a healthy relationship must be built on honesty and trust, then jealousy must be kept in check.

The first way to do this is to own our emotions and deal with our inner critic rather than allowing it to poison our relationship. We should work hard to be vulnerable and open to our partner, to offer them our trust and support for their independence and individuality. This doesn't mean we have to agree to an open relationship. Rather, it means working on having open communication and trying not to allow our inner critic to overtake us and drive our behavior.

Anxiety is something else that can lead to disagreements. You and your Queen may be happily engaging in hotwifing, but you begin to feel anxious that your relationship could fall apart. Anxiety can lead you to create distance between you and your partner. At its worst, your anxiety can even push us to give up on love altogether. Being in a relationship and falling in love challenges us in numerous ways we don't expect. The more we value someone else, the more we stand to lose. On many levels, both conscious and unconscious, we become scared of being hurt.

When we are in relationships, it isn't only the issues that occur between us and our partner that make us anxious. It's the things we tell ourselves about what's going on. This is called "the critical voice." This critical inner voice makes us turn against ourselves and the people close to us. It can promote hostile, paranoid, and suspicious thinking that lowers our self-esteem and drives unhealthy levels of distrust, defensiveness, jealousy, and anxiety. Basically, it feeds us a consistent stream of thoughts that undermine our happiness and make us worry about our relationship, rather than just enjoying it.

The issue with anxiety and having open relationships hotwifing is there are added factors to deal with which may not be in the open because neither you nor your partner wants to kill the vibe. If you suppress the feelings of anxiety, you could start to act out in destructive ways, making nasty comments or becoming childish or parental toward your significant other. If it continues, you've completely shifted the dynamic between the two of you. Instead of enjoying the time you have together, you may waste an entire night feeling withdrawn and upset with each other. You've now effectively forced the distance you initially feared.

The critical inner voice tends to terrorize and catastrophize reality. It can rouse serious spells of anxiety about dynamics that don't exist and threats that aren't even tangible. Know what you want in your ideal open relationship. What do you think hotwifing will bring to your life? What challenges do you imagine you will face, and can you handle them? Do you have enough time in your world for multiple partners? Do you want to have the time, energy, and availability for more people? What does your Queen want and are you looking for the same sort of open relationship? Are you open to doing for her what she wants, even if you don't get what you want?

The defenses we form from the critical voices we hear are based on our own unique experiences and adaptations. When we feel anxious or insecure, some of us tend to become clingy and desperate in our actions. We may feel possessive or controlling toward our partner in response. Conversely, some of us will feel easily intruded on in our relationships. We may retreat from our partners, detach from our feelings of desire. We may act out by being aloof, distant, or guarded. This behavior can lead to disagreements that threaten the bond of the primary relationship. That study, published in the *Journal of Family Psychology,* highlights the fact that the way you engage with your partner affects your overall well-being in many ways. How you treat your partner will affect how well you communicate.

Creating and maintaining a sustaining intimate relationship isn't easy. But it is something you can practice. You and your partner can examine and reveal how you each experience your own self within the relationship. How do you see your own life "evolution" over the years? Are you in sync with each other's vision of life together? If there are gaps, how will you address them and deal with them? Answering these questions can help with disagreements. Douglas LaBier, a psychologist, talks about "radical transparency," which can help couples assess such questions openly and honestly, which includes the following description of the two parts of radical transparency:

- Being open and revealing yourself to your partner. This means letting go of inhibitions or defensive feelings you might be harboring about what you haven't revealed and also acknowledging your reluctance to do so.

- Being open and receptive to *your partner's* reality—his or her feelings, wishes, desires, fears, and differences from yourself. It means openly encouraging your partner to express these to you.

He believes that Radical Transparency can put you on the path to strengthening the foundation of your relationship, which can go a long way to reducing disagreements.

Studies show that stress can arise in relationships when partners experience conflicting goals, motives, and preferences. Common sources of conflict involve unmet expectations, intimacy, time spent together, financial difficulties, discrepancies in equity and power, domestic and family responsibilities, parenting, jealousy, bad habits, and more. Unresolved conflicts and the stress associated with conflict put even the most satisfying relationship at risk.

Moreover, managing and resolving conflict is difficult and can be a significant source of stress. Indeed, one of the most pressing problems couples identify is how to communicate while resolving their disagreements, and relationship therapists agree that dysfunctional communication is the most damaging and difficult to treat relationship problems. Identifying what constitutes effective communication during conflict is thus critical to help couples resolve issues and sustain their relationships.

Chapter 24

Keep the Primary Relationship Alive

When people complain about being bored in their relationship, they often cite being stuck in a rut or routine. Then there is the worry about how to keep the relationship alive. They may feel a sudden desire for novelty and assume that novelty can only come from a new partner. One of the biggest issues with hotwifing is the tendency for the primary relationship to begin to break down. All the focus goes to the hotwifing experience, and the primary relationship can become mundane and insignificant. Here are a few tips on how to keep the primary relationship between you and your Queen strong:

Re-Enforce Your Relationship Daily

Remind her of the love you both feel daily. Kiss, hug, and greet her as the Queen and don't allow the relationship to take a backseat. In our busy world, we tend to place things above the relationship, and only when going out do we make a big deal. We make excuses for being busy, tired, or just not in the mood. Now more than ever, you both will need to spend time on the relationship.

Take Care of Your Health and Fitness

Often so much is going on that we barely have time to worry about the upkeep of our health and fitness. Only when you are healthy and feel good about yourself can you take care of your partner. So, remember to eat right, stay fit, and sleep well. A healthy body results in a healthy mind and that clearly reflects in your relationship. Remain attractive to both of you. This increases the sexiness of all other activities.

Spend Time Together

While adding in hotwifing it is important to spend quality time together with just the two of you. Going out with the kids is not considered quality time together. You still need a date night and maybe picnics in the park, bike rides, or just hanging out. I can recall a couple who was married for 27 years and introduced all sorts of extras into their relationship, but they had lunch together every single day to just talk. It worked. Their relationship was able to withstand any obstacle.

Give Your Queen Space

Being in a relationship doesn't mean that you have to be together every second of the day. She still needs to meet with her friends, and you still need the beer night with the boys. Allow each other to have the time to spend alone as well.

Help with Chores

There is a reason why 80 percent of women complain about being too tired to have sex or do anything. Women have to excel in their careers, take care of the kids, take care of the household, and their man's needs. It's an exhausting life. Any support you give to your Queen will help her and keep her in a sexier mood.

Make Her Feel Special

Every day is an opportunity to make your Queen feel special. You have so many chances to compliment her, leave her love notes, bring her flowers and make her feel like she is the luckiest person in the world. Not only will she be in a better mood, but she will also respond in a positive way, and it keeps the focus on you and not the hotwifing as much. The truth is, every interaction we have with another person, even someone we've known for a long time, is a new possibility for lively connection. It often takes only a small action—a sweet smile, a flirtatious look, or an act of affection to turn a mundane interaction into an exciting one. These are simple ways to make your Queen feel special. Check her out and give her that sensual look like she is the most gorgeous woman on the planet.

Keep Touching

Touch is so important in relationships. Whether it's kissing, handholding, hugging, or cuddling, all keep the spice alive. Touch her hair, her back, and her legs often. Squeeze her butt as you go by. Give her a kiss for no reason and hold hands. Touch keeps the focus on you both.

Set the Scene

Just like you would prepare for your big night of hotwifing, you also need to keep the primary space sexy. Draw her a bath, lay out some lingerie, get her favorite bubbles, some wine or champagne, and massage oils. You want to show dedication and effort. Men always complain that they don't understand why women are upset. Women want the fantasy without having to explain each and every step. You will want to show this woman that even though you engage in open relationships, the primary relationship is what you need. Make a delicious dinner with candlelight for her. There is no need to wait for a special moment to make her feel loved.

Have Sex Regularly

Your sex life still needs to be great and regular. Hotwifing is not going to fix a boring sex life or any other issues in the relationship. So, it is crucial that you have a great sex life and keep it alive. You can reserve certain acts for hotwifing while engaging in others in your intimate times. For example, you can reserve oral and anal sex for your own sex times. It is recommended that having sex is integral for connecting deeply as a couple.

Be Truthful

Studies have found that people who are truthful about themselves experience more relationship intimacy and well-being, and better romantic relationships. Overall, studies find that positive connection and intimacy grow when you are transparent about what's inside of you. A recent study by the University of Georgia observed the connection between communication and the degree of satisfaction reported by couples. It found that good communication could not account for how satisfied partners were with a relationship over time.

The researchers recognize that other factors must influence couples' satisfaction, and that good communication can result from those factors. According to Justin Lavner, lead author of the study, discovered that more-satisfied couples communicate better on average than those who are less satisfied. So, what is going to make you and your Queen more satisfied is the happiness you feel together and being truthful and honest about your feelings throughout your exploration.

CHAPTER 25

A Woman's Needs in an Open Relationship

Women will always be the ones to be criticized in an open relationship so their needs must be honored. Men have always had the freedom to do what they want—cheat, have threesomes, crave hotwifing, and do group sex, but if a woman admits to doing this, she is labeled "a whore," "unstable," or "a sex maniac." Today, times are changing. Women are demanding to have the same right to do what they want with their lives and relationships. They require you to be open and supportive in the adventure, if it's to go well.

Here are some of the things women need. They have the right, without shame, blame, or guilt in all intimate relationships, to be free from male coercion, male violence, and male intimidation. They should be able to choose how they want to conduct themselves in open relationships. Women have the need to explore their emotions and communicate all of their feminine needs as they set the rules and boundaries, which are to be respected by you if you have consented to an open relationship.

They need to know that you are on board to satisfy their needs in sex and hotwifing and you will be supportive no matter what happens. Why is this important? Because men will criticize women for having this much control. In a Female Led Relationship, it is the woman who decides how many partners she wants and the level of time and investment and what sexual pleasures she will offer to each male partner. Although she is leading, she will do so in a loving and compassionate way and will discuss openly with you and anyone else involved.

Your role as the primary male is to "wait at home," pursue a "non-sexual experience" or spend time with friends, while she goes out. You will learn to do your best to overcome your desire to control the situation during her outings. You must accept your role and duty as her supporter. If you feel fearful, jealous, panicked, or some other unpleasant emotion, you must communicate this to your Queen, so you can work it out.

It is in the sole discretion of the Queen as a female leader whether you will also be allowed to have relationships with outside connections. As the male primary partner, you will always respect her command and follow her direction in all cases. For example, if you are both on vacation and she decides she wants to explore with another man, then you can discuss how it will unfold, but she will ultimately lead in how it unfolds. She makes the first move and directs you.

The Queen will be free to make commitments and accept responsibility for her actions. Her freedom comes from the personal expression of her own power. No one can take away the female's power to be herself and to lead the relationship. The *Love & Obey* female chooses freely to help empower her man partner, not to humiliate him or abuse him. She chooses to love, honor, and respect in exchange for your 100 percent absolute obedience to her will.

As you have read, this book is for couples who are deeply committed to one another and choose to embark on shared sexually open experiences with outside individuals. These open experiences will set aside the traditional rules of a monogamous relationship or marriage. I have shown you that you need to promise to each other to be open, honest, and loyal at all times during this experience. Under no circumstances, will you lie or mislead one another. Your Queen will need to trust you and herself.

Chapter 26

The Rules for a Female Led Relationship

In a Female Led Relationship, the rules for hotwifing are skewed to give the female complete control but there are still some things that can be done to ensure a smooth experience. The following are the keys to hotwifing in a Female Led Relationship.

Key # 1. Both partners must deal with feelings of jealousy

It is natural to feel possessive and jealous in the few times you are embarking in hotwifing. The way for you to deal with jealousy is to understand why you are engaging in hotwifing and ensure that you and your Queen are on the same page.

You may have the inclination to say the following:

"I'm jealous. I don't look like those hot guys you were checking out."

"I got really jealous when you went down on my girlfriend like that."

"I'm feeling a little jealous and trying to get through it."

"I know you love me, but I need some reassurance."

The minute you say, "I'm jealous," out loud, it stops being a negative and destructive force and becomes a signal to your partner that you need some attention and reinforcement. The key to getting past these feelings is to address them in an open fashion. You and your Queen need to be understanding and patient through the process and be willing to abort if it seems too overwhelming. Hence the need to do everything together.

The key to being in a Female Led Relationship is that while this may be something initiated for your Queen's pleasure, you need to be 100 percent in agreement. There is no point in lying or trying to hide your feelings as these will lead to resentment and destruction of your relationship. If you are having these feelings, you must refrain from outbursts and displays of anger. Know that this is something that can be resolved in a peaceful manner.

Whatever you and Queen decide to do, whether insisting on monogamy or making certain exceptions, that is for them alone to decide. What matters is that once you've decided and agreed upon the terms of your relationship, you must stand by these decisions. In doing so, you offer trust, freedom, and respect as the separate individuals they are. When two people recognize each other's individuality, they're able to avoid falling into a fake bond, which is an illusion of connection that replaces real love and sabotages exciting relationships. They're able to maintain their attractions to each other and to keep the spark alive, so to speak.

All couples should strive to be honest with each other, deal with their jealous feelings in healthy ways, and challenge their deeply rooted fears of intimacy to avoid a fake bond and other traps that doom relationships. By making this their focus, they are far better able to sustain richer, more rewarding relationships. They are much better equipped to have open, honest, and mature discussions about attractions and monogamy and are much less likely to engage in deception and secret infidelity.

Key # 2. You both reinforce your love

There is a reason you and your Queen are in a relationship. There is love. It takes real love to want to see your partner very happy and what is necessary to ensure you serve your Queen. Therefore, the key to successful hotwifing is to remember and reinforce love as the primary partner in your relationship. No one can destroy a strong bond made of real love. Your desire to explore does not diminish your love for each other. So, celebrate it.

Hotwifing can make you feel like you are not enough to satisfy her, which can spark a huge ego flare-up in some men. They take it as they are not worthy, good enough, or manly enough to satisfy the Queen. But the truth is women can love you and just need some outside experience. How many men have said cheating did not really matter—that it was just sex?

The same is for your Queen, who may have the desire for hotwifing. It doesn't mean she loves you less or more. She loves you. She doesn't want you to change "or fix" anything about you. She wants you fully in her life and not on the sidelines. She wants you right there, in the inner fold of her female passion and her loving authority. You need to know that when she has a sexual attraction to someone else or a romantic connection with someone else, it neither invalidates your love nor lessens what she feels for you. In fact, it can make her love you more because you understand she has needs.

Key # 3. Your Queen makes the rules

She leads your relationship, and you must obey her, but you may feel the need to confront her about a major issue like taking on a new lover. However, you should be a team player with her. Do not be disobedient or back her into a corner, as that will be a mistake.

"We're not getting out of this car until we talk."

"You're not leaving this house until we talk."

Don't say things like that to her. That is disobedient and backing her into a corner. You don't corner your Mistress and demand conversation. You don't make ultimatums. You don't withhold your services, sexual, or otherwise because she is not doing what you want. She is in charge and has every right to do what she wants. You made the choice to be in a Female Led Relationship, and it is not for you to decide.

Look at it like your "partners-in-love" co-workers hatching a new project. You're both teammates with a new "big game" coming up. Look at it like, you're doing this together. Sometimes you will have to pick up the slack. Sometimes they'll have to pick up the slack. When there's a problem, cornering a teammate, a co-worker, or a life partner and making demands are not the best way to work things out. Instead, talk things out and plan out this new adventure together.

Key # 4. Do everything together

I have stressed this for a reason. The couples who play together stay together. These adventures are just that—exploration, and they must be done together with the consent of all parties involved. You and your Queen make the decisions together of how to engage in many forms of open relationships so you can respect your relationship. Your main relationship takes priority, and all other adventures, including hotwifing, should be done together.

Key # 5: Be loving and kind

Scientists have made efforts to classify different types of love. Recently, researcher Dr. Barbara Acevedo discovered some good news about one type in particular. "Romantic love," the kind that is characterized by "intensity, engagement, and sexual interest" can last a lifetime.

Neuroscientists have even discovered that the brains of couples who experience this kind of love can keep firing for each other the same way they did when they first met 20 or so years later. Romantic love is associated with marital satisfaction, well-being, high self-esteem, and relationship longevity. You want to invest in building romantic love by being loving.

In Female Led Relationships, we are dealing with strong dominant women who do what they want and the men who submit to their desires. For many couples, the man's ego and pride are still a factor, and sometimes he doesn't want to know, even though he knows. So, we can be driven to be mean and critical out of emotions we may feel while engaging in hotwifing. However, I think open and honest communication is the key to a long-term successful open relationship. I think couples should show loving kindness.

When we meet someone new it is easy to feel what scientists Elaine Hatfield and Richard Rapson describe as passionate love, which they state is "a state of intense longing for union with another." But there can be an obsessive element, characterized by intrusive thinking, uncertainty, and mood swings. So, this type of love can work well at the beginning of relationships but can be hurtful in the long run. During hotwifing, it is easy to feel swept away by the newness of it all, but it will be extremely important to focus on the real love—the romantic love you have between you and the Queen.

Kindness was found to be the most imperative characteristic in a relationship. It beat out physical attractiveness, good financial prospects, humor, chastity, religiosity, the desire for children, and creativity. Kindness is defined as the quality of being friendly, generous, and considerate. When we have negative views of ourselves, it's challenging to be kind toward others. If we lack self-compassion and have harsh, judgmental attitudes toward ourselves, we extend those same feelings toward others. Therefore, it is necessary to start with being kind to yourself. Once you are happy with yourself, this will transfer to your partner. Kindness to your Queen and vice versa is one of the greatest gifts you can give each other.

Chapter 27

Alternative Forms of Hotwifing

Hotwifing Alone

The main suggestion in this book was that both men and women should partake in hotwifing together. This ensures that the relationship stays sound and both people feel involved. But sometimes the Queen decides that she wants to see the Bull alone. You may want to ask yourself if the encounter should occur and what the safeguards are. In the show *Succession*, Shiv Roy decides that she wants to see men outside of the relationship and she does this without the presence of her husband. While this can leave you feeling ignored and left out, it can be a critical evolution to allow her to do it.

First, it establishes trust. If you cannot trust her to carry this out and return to you, there is an issue in the relationship. By allowing her to have the freedom, you are giving her complete loyalty and devotion. However, this kind of freedom must be done responsibly. It will be important to review the rules, and of course, have a discussion after. Many couples may have an intimate moment after the Queen returns home to maintain a bond. In this scenario, it may be important to agree that only certain acts will be allowed and others are forbidden. If she sticks to the rules then allowing her the freedom to do it alone, may not be such a bad thing. Couples tend to enjoy hotwifing alone when the man craves to only hear about the acts and not actually be a part of it.

Another scenario where hotwifing occurs alone is where the Queen is a unicorn for swinging couples. This is perfectly acceptable as well, as long as you give your consent and are happy to sit back and watch. The important thing to note is that no one person should feel ignored, so in this scenario, your Queen should only engage in hotwifing if you both agree it is something you desire. It goes without saying that she should never engage with one part of a swinging couple alone.

Hotwifing with a Woman

Most hotwifing encounters involve another man, the Bull, who is generally more well-endowed. But sometimes the hotwifing is done with a woman. Some men think this is the best of both worlds because they assume it will be a threesome. But generally, hotwifing with a woman will not be done together with you, so it could have some challenges. One of the main rules is the outside partner or Bull should never be someone you could develop an emotional relationship with. Does this include your Queen developing a relationship with a woman and developing a friendship?

It will be important to review the rules and ensure the strength of the primary relationship. If hotwifing is to happen with a woman, there should be clear boundaries established and no development of an emotional bond. This also applies to you attempting to meet the outside woman as well. There are all sorts of ways this could go wrong.

Hotwifing Followed by Sex with the Queen

In some hotwifing relationships, there is a desire for the man to show his devotion by performing sex with the Queen after she has been with the Bull. This is perfectly acceptable as long as your Queen desires to do this. Sometimes couples see this as a way of bonding after their extracurricular activity. Again, it is perfectly acceptable.

Engage in Hotwifing as Punishment

Many times in relationships, we can get furious and say things we do not mean. So, it would be very easy to use hotwifing as a threat to a man. Your Queen may say, "I'm going to sleep with another man because I am frustrated with you." While arguments do happen and people can exchange angry words, Hotwifing should never be used to punish.

First of all, doing so violates the important trust in the relationship where men and women must give their consent. If it is used as punishment, you can be left with a very negative feeling, which can lead to harboring ill feelings. Where hotwifing should be adding excitement and adventure to the relationship, it should not add fear and dishonesty. This takes things too far into the cheating realm. Left unchecked, this could turn out into a way you hurt each other and the relationship.

Engaging in Hotwifing with Another Couple

This may seem like it's the same as wife swapping but it's not. Hotwifing with another couple could consist of you watching while she is with two other men, she is with a man and a woman, or she is with two other women. All of these are options, but they do come with their own challenges.

Now it's more important to ensure there are no feelings of jealousy or being left out. You should fully discuss with her how it will unfold and what each of your roles will be. You will have to be particularly okay with how the man and woman engage with your Queen and stick to the rules and boundaries. Perhaps there is no oral sex received or given. Maybe there will only be one act being performed at one time or everyone is participating. These alternatives should only be done once you are successful with the simple version. The more partners, the more you might have to deal with.

Today, more than 50 percent of couples have a cheating spouse and many end in divorce, so the old ways are not working. Blame new lifestyles, a society that wants instant pleasure or a change in values. But something has to change. Hotwifing could be an answer to some of the issues leading to infidelity, and there seems to be less lying, deceit, and dishonesty by lovers and life partners, whether married or in a committed relationship.

A relationship that is exciting, loving, honest, and filled with trust should be the new standard. For me, trust is the most important rarest and most difficult quality to maintain in a long-term relationship, especially one that involves sex with more than one person. No matter the controversy, hotwifing is here to stay. Couples love hotwifing. Men are requesting it and women are loving it. Many couples are changing the dynamic in relationships because they are looking for variety and many are looking to fulfill inner needs. There are very few relationships that break up over hotwifing.

Conclusion

Hotwifing is becoming one of the most fascinating sexual activities in relationships, and there is growing interest in it from both men and women. Today, hotwifing is more than just sex. There can be complex issues at play, and quite often, men and women are both interested in exploring it. Today, relationships are dramatically different than they were even 20 years ago. The divorce rate is still around 50 percent, and infidelity, lying, and dishonesty play a huge role in the destruction of many relationships.

Hotwifing can be a game changer because it offers the opportunity for excitement and exploration with consent. Everyone involved is aware and is in agreement. Hotwifing is different because the woman is in control. She is the center and main attraction, not some side dish to be added to the play. In this regard, a Queen who wants to be a hotwife has the advantage of doing so, right alongside her spouse and any other consenting adult. Hotwifing falls under consensual non-monogamy and ethical non-monogamy. Consensual non-monogamy involves couples who are married or in long-term relationships but seek to have external sexual encounters with the permission and agreement of their primary partner.

So, you and your Queen are married but you both make a decision to explore mostly casual encounters with others. As part of understanding hotwifing, we need to look at women's experience of sex and sexual intimacy at different ages and phases of life. People often think that women only seem keen to have sex when they're younger and perhaps as far as their mid-thirties. This is a complete misconception as women describe having the desire for sex throughout all phases of life. The only difference is that the type of sex and the interaction can change.

Right from the start, a woman who engages in hotwifing with her partner fully supporting it has the best of both worlds. She receives sexual pleasure, which she may not have had previously, and she has her husband or boyfriend serving her like a Queen. So, the woman is really in the power position. There are those who will criticize, but how a couple chooses to build excitement in their lives is completely up to them. Many have reported a closer bond with their partners because, unlike cheating, they are open and upfront about everything that happens. With both partners in agreement, the couple can control how far they will take their activities.

Hotwifing can be the fulfillment of a fantasy. Other times, it's more than that. He wants to show his Queen his devotion. He derives sexual satisfaction from knowing that he is in service to his woman, and she is still his Queen. The man still feels like he's in control because he wants to see his Queen with a man who is better able to satisfy her. It places men in a much more alpha and powerful position than cuckolding where the goal is humiliation. Most alpha men still want to serve a powerful woman, and many have a deep desire to show great service to her, even though they are strong and powerful in their own lives. Hotwifing has been shown to improve relationships with better communication, honesty, better sex, deeper bonds, and improved self-esteem and confidence.

Made in the USA
Las Vegas, NV
18 March 2022